~ *Decorative* ~
# Dolls' Houses

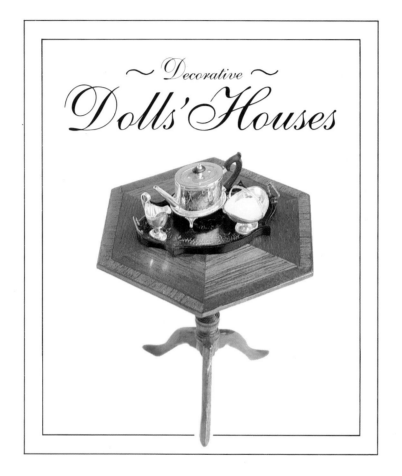

~ *Decorative* ~

Dolls' Houses

ORIGINAL INTERIORS FOR TWENTY FIVE DOLLS' HOUSES

~ *Caroline Hamilton* ~

CRESCENT BOOKS

NEW YORK · AVENEL, NEW JERSEY

Jane

SINE QUA NON

❦

First published in the UK in 1990 by Ebury Press

Commissioned photographs copyright © 1990 Ebury Press Ltd

Text copyright © 1990 Caroline Hamilton

This 1994 edition published by
Crescent Books, distributed by
Outlet Book Company, Inc.,
a Random House Company
40 Engelhard Avenue
Avenel, New Jersey 07001

Random House

New York · Toronto · London · Sydney · Auckland

Editors: Gillian Haslam and Emma Callery
Designer: Harry Green   Photographer: Jon Stewart

ISBN 0-517-10242-0

Filmset in Baskerville by Advanced Filmsetters (Glasgow) Ltd
Printed and bound in Italy by New Interlitho, S.p.a., Milan

A finely detailed, hand-raised sterling silver tea set in the
Georgian 1790s style by Stuart McCabe is featured on page 1. Black and
gold tray by Alan Waters. Hexagonal table by Malcolm Chandler.

*T*he Victorian House, *previous page*, is described on page 26,
built over several years of attending 'Woodwork for beginners' adult
education classes.

❦

Contents

Foreword

*D*rawing room of the Georgian town house
shown on page 104. The furniture shows fine work by
several different British craftsmen.

*I*n the final quarter of the twentieth century, the extraordinary renaissance of interest in miniaturiana, especially in Britain and the United States, has been a veritable explosion.

Attics have been plundered of antique dolls' houses which had gathered cobwebs for generations, and their values have vaulted, as those of most antiques have, to astonishing heights. The most flourishing area of miniature activity, however, has been in the creating of newly-built dolls' houses, shops, rooms and related buildings, by both beginners and collectors, furnished both by craftsmen and Taiwan, and the selection is multitudinous.

What is not available, the ingenious author of *Decorative Dolls' Houses* has either created herself or is prepared to create, to share her felicitous solutions to miniature problems with the miniature world.

Collectors of miniaturiana, like all collectors, come in many flavours. Most are reproducing period houses, eighteenth or nineteenth century, reflecting the nostalgia which has seized many of the world's wistful citizens.

Some of these collectors are discriminating. More of them are, to employ a euphemism, eclectic. Many of them are confused – confused about period, or about how to begin, or how to proceed, or whether to proceed at all. Caroline Hamilton's appealing book performs a tremendous service for all of them.

She is the perfect cicerone for the most discriminating, but her houses, and her words, cannot fail to help those who flounder as well. Her book is a lovely blend of historical background and practical information accomplished, as her creations are, with wit, warmth and style. Her book will unquestionably become the standard work for dolls' house decorators. It is surprisingly readable even for those of us who are not quite certain about what to do with a pot of glue or, even which glue to use.

FLORA GILL JACOBS
Washington Dolls' House and Toy Museum
5236 44th Street, N.W., Washington DC 20015
USA

There are such people as polymaths, and in her own sphere I should name Caroline Hamilton as belonging to that rare group: to be an inspired electrician (dolls' houses in mind) and an organiser of the enormous London Dolls' House Festival, by now of international reputation, is in itself a fair step towards the awe with which one regards the all-round accomplishments of a polymath.

Long ago, just after World War II, in New York I met a man who was perhaps the first and most outstanding maker of miniature objects for dolls' houses. Down in a basement, I seem to remember, was an array of entrancing objects of a kind I had never seen or imagined: I bought a ship in a glass bottle one inch long containing a fully rigged sailing ship, 'made by a nun' I was told.

I so wished that one could buy such exquisite artifacts in England but at that time there were unregarded, unvalued, Victorian and earlier dolls' house furnishings to be bought, and these soon became an exclusive passion. The pale blue milk-glass vases, the old imported Thuringian furniture, the blue and white dinner services in scale, bedsteps, looking glasses, all these were fondly collected at a cost of ten shillings each. Now, in the London Dolls' House Festival, modern craftsmen have an outlet for their exquisitely skillful handwork that is possibly the largest and most joyful venue for collector. May it long continue for our delight.

VIVIEN GREENE
The Rotunda Private Dolls' House Museum
Grove House, Iffley Turn, Oxford OX4 4HN,
England

Introduction

Dolls' houses for grown-ups? Yes! This is a perfectly respectable hobby for both men and women that has been around for centuries as the magnificent examples of seventeenth-century artistry in Dutch and German Museums will testify.

Very early collections were often housed in handsome pieces of furniture, hence the name Cabinet Houses. They had room settings and even stables and gardens fitted into compartments behind inlaid doors that bore no external resemblance to houses. Sometimes gardens were ingeniously arranged in a drawer below the main cupboard.

As early as the beginning of the eighteenth century there were 'Baby Houses' with windows and doors in their façades. These usually had locks on their opening fronts to guard their precious contents. Fascinating bills and inventories survive which show that collectors spent as liberally then on exquisite miniature silver, porcelain and furniture as their modern counterparts do now.

These Baby Houses followed a convention of only being one room deep and sometimes their staircases vanished abruptly after a grand opening flourish on the ground floor. In other respects, though, they depict contemporary life with charming and instructive accuracy, like the pictorial laundry list for illiterate servants in the Nürenberg National Museum in Germany, or the glass dishes suspended over candle sconces to protect the ceilings from smoke in Uppark in England.

My love of dolls' houses began as a child when my mother made me simple furniture out of matchboxes and cotton reels and I slowly gained sufficient

Gothic castle built by Samuel Halfpenny using polished hardwoods and decorated by Jane in the style of Augustus Pugin (see pages 54–9). A Pugin stained-glass design was photocopied onto acetate to be coloured by hand for the chapel window.

dexterity to make things myself. The interest stayed with me and grew as I visited museums in many countries that have collections of dolls' houses and old toys. I must declare an abiding enthusiasm for anything miniature: I am equally prepared to gasp at wondrously delicate ivory antiques, to be interested in the provenance of early manufactured houses and furniture, to smile at home-made clumsy pieces, and to giggle over toy pink plastic telephones. There is an irresistible charm about real-life rendered small that transcends any minor defects in execution.

'Miniatures' have been made in a variety of scales ranging from 1/10th and a rather heavy looking 1/12th in old dolls' houses, through much smaller scales for furniture made all in silver, ivory or filigree pressed metal. Some early twentieth-century manufacturers used the 1/16th scale which is still prevalent in mass production pieces in Britain and Europe. The 1/12th scale is now the European standard for the serious hobby, although items intended for children still come in a bewildering variety of sizes.

In America the 1/12th scale has been usual, both for craftsmen-made pieces and imported Far Eastern manufactured goods. However, in recent years there has been a strong trend to half as small again in 1/24th or even smaller as keen collectors found their real houses filling up at an alarming rate with ever more ambitious four-sided mansions.

Other authors have written the standard works on antique dolls' houses, which I have read with great pleasure, and there have been many books on making dolls' houses and their contents. The problem is that some of the instructions are useful some of the time to some of the readers, but in a hobby that encompasses so many different crafts from carpentry through sewing to silversmithing and glassblowing, it is impossible to pitch 'how to' instructions at a level which will not daunt some and frustrate others.

This book shows just how much fun can be had in collecting, converting, improving and making dolls' houses and their contents. I have been lucky enough to have a great friend and hobby soul mate, Jane, to share my enthusiasm. During our home-making and child-rearing years we both acquired 'Mrs Average' manual skills and find that these can be applied in miniature with great satisfaction. We both have an abiding interest in full-size interior decoration, we read widely and visit museums and historic houses with the constant theme 'Oh, wouldn't that be lovely in miniature' running through our minds.

So I commend you to look at real houses and their contents and to absorb styles and differing tastes by keen observation of the real thing. Use your own talents to make miniatures in that field, be brave at having a go at new skills, get yourself out of trouble by cunning adaptation, but don't worry about giving in gracefully if you find that others can do something better. After all, in real life we don't expect to be able to build, plumb, wire and furnish our homes single-handedly either.

English high Victorian architecture in a house by Derrick Piper. The brick and stone work are built up with plaster compound and individually painted.

Scottish artist's house: built by Kevin Mulvany from 1901 drawings by Charles Rennie Mackintosh for a house that was never built in real life.

French maison de ville (*opposite*): built by Kevin Mulvany from the central section of a design for a larger French town house with details from a real house in Versailles. The real wrought iron balcony was faithfully copied by John Watkins.

This book offers a guided tour around 25 varied houses and shops giving you the background story and pointing out aspects of the hobby that they illustrate. I am delighted that there are so many full page pictures to allow you to see the dolls' houses clearly but you might still find it useful to have a magnifying glass to hand in order to blow up the details even further. The last section provides practical help and useful tips and guidance to help you create your own projects.

Whether you choose to have dolls in your miniature settings or not is up to you, but to my mind there should always be at least an imaginary inhabitant whose tastes and comfort is catered for, otherwise we would just be talking about model-making and not about dolls' houses.

Wish Fulfilment in Miniature

The fine houses shown on these pages have been chosen for their great variety in style, to delight and inspire. They are far removed from children's toys, although some people may prefer the more direct, naive appeal of the small dolls' houses that retain an element of childlike simplicity. On the other hand,

American Regency period house in Washington DC, once inhabited by President Alexander Grant. Copied by Bernardo Traettino, one of the pioneer builders of realistic dolls' houses for adult collectors in Britain.

a very strong factor in the appeal of the dolls' house hobby to the adult collector is the element of wish fulfilment. Sometimes even a new entrant into the hobby might feel that they just want the very best, to start as they mean to go on. It may well not be possible to live in a beautiful Georgian mansion in real life; but it is certainly possible to fulfil your dreams of grandeur in small scale. What is more, you can engage a whole household of domestic help to look after your miniature self, your miniature family will never talk back or disobey you, and absolutely no one will complain if you move all the furniture around for a third time in one day!

A keen collector whose standards have worked their way up from simple beginnings might be nursing a great longing to possess the ultimate house for them. State of the art dolls' houses are rarely to be seen for sale in a shop as they cost a great deal of money, even if there is no such thing as a rich dolls' house builder. A commission for a house of this kind will require a great deal of thought and the collector will have to form very definite views on the period and style that attracts them most. The dolls' house hobby can lead its adherents into a host of rewarding byways. Detailed research into architectural features can give rise to interesting reading and even journeys to see full size examples of the sort of house you would like to portray in miniature. The history of every facet of interior decoration, the dating of domestic equipment and of costume and hairstyles all ramify into a never ending quest for period accuracy.

These houses may also serve as an introduction to the high level of skill and devoted workmanship that are involved in dolls' houses for the kind of person who already has great skills in full size and simply had not realized that there is such scope for applying their craftsmanship in this hobby. There are many examples of artisans who have left full size architecture, cabinet making, glass blowing or silversmithing to work in small scale. Their work is very much sought after by a growing number of discriminating collectors throughout the world. However, the middle ground is well served by mass production, mostly in the Far East, which in turn is growing in sophistication and variety. The artisans working on their own have therefore to find their market through originality of concept and top quality in execution. I would be delighted to think that this book might attract more talents into the field.

The majority of collectors will be those of us who potter happily with our modest dolls' houses, knowing that it would take more spare money than we're ever likely to have to commission such splendid mansions, or several lifetimes to acquire the expertise of top artisans. I do hope, however, that readers will remember that although the various dolls' houses shown here may appear to be very grand, they are, after all, only made by one pair of hands. That is something we all share, so all we need is the patience to learn and the will to make the best of what talents we have. In this, time is both an enemy and a friend. It is, of course, a constant source of frustration that many of our modern lives are too hectic and demanding to allow us to devote many hours to a hobby. However, to look at it another way, even a little free time is just that: free. We have the most precious asset that every skilled craftsperson wishes he or she could double. As amateurs, we are under no obligation to meet any deadlines and we can give our projects the tender loving care that will make up for any initial lack of skill.

Where to Begin

If you are an absolute beginner, my advice is: don't rush out and blow the budget on a house! Wait until you've seen the full range of what is available both in period styles and do-it-yourself versus ready-made or special commissions. Give your own ideas time to evolve. You can enjoy yourself looking around and there's no need to resist the temptation to buy a few little accessories while you're doing so, they're bound to find a home somewhere, but do let your ideas simmer and bubble for a while before you make a major

Forever England

BRYAN POOL
PLUCKLEY   1987

purchase. Not easy advice to take as almost every collector friend I have has a 'first effort', blushing somewhere in a corner, testifying to enthusiasm rather than discrimination.

Why not eye your full-size house for possibilities? Bookshelves are ideal for a temporary room setting: push some books aside and the resulting niche will be a good size to display a few miniatures in the most popular 1/12th, or inch to the foot, craftsmen's scale. You can go a step further and cut three cardboard or foam-core walls to paper or paint.

I have a friend who found this sort of setting so attractive she never did progress to a house. She has a miniature drawing room in her full-size living room display shelves, the small study is among the books of her real study, she has a little three-sided kitchen on her kitchen window sill, and a bathroom cabinet has lost a door to reveal a mini bathroom. This is also the irrefutable answer to someone who protests that they haven't got room for a dolls' house.

In your own home you may have a suitable cabinet or be willing to sacrifice the pigeon holes in a desk or even a treasure such as an old scientific instrument case or an old clock case in which to start. Dolls' house room boxes can be made from anything remotely correct in scale, it doesn't matter if it's a bright blue plastic storage box laid on its side – it will look quite different once you've had a go at it. My Grandmamma's parlour (page 102) started life as a Harrods' food box. All I did was to tip it up and replace the sliding wooden lid with a sheet of glass with its edges safely polished. Making small vignettes or instant settings of this kind might give you the confidence you need to start on a more ambitious project and it will certainly give you invaluable hands-on experience. Instructions for building boxes are given on pages 101–3.

Room boxes can be as elaborate as you like in their interior decoration and exterior finish. Concealed lighting, false walls, vistas through windows, illusions of perspective can all come into play, almost more than in a dolls' house; they can be like designing a stage setting.

Very sophisticated collectors use them for one-off projects like an exercise in a particular style or like the historically accurate reconstruction of a room in a palace, where the whole building would obviously swamp their real home if carried out in the 1/12th scale.

However, if you are just longing to have a whole house, I don't suppose you will hold back for long, so having had a good look round I would just say: be guided by your heart. Fall in love and plump for the house that is right for you. You will be putting a lot of time and effort into it, so go for a style that you know about and can spontaneously interpret in miniature. Your own recollections, taste, specialized knowledge or sense of humour will then help you add all the little details which will make it look right.

Tudor Mansion built by the late Bryan Pool of 'Forever England' who specialized in using authentic building methods and materials like individual hand-made bricks and roof tiles.

Houses

$\mathcal{T}$his is a guided tour of many dolls' houses looking at different eras and styles, following my evolution as a collector and maker. I hope to encourage you to enjoy yourself as much as I have.

On the *previous page* is the interior of the thatched cottage described on page 44. Much of the charm of this house depends on the mood created by soft candlelight and the warm glow emanating from the open hearths. The furniture is mostly oak in mid-eighteenth-century styles.

This is the interior of an Edwardian villa (left) that comes as a kit from Honeychurch Toys. The stairs were omitted to gain space and the drawing room has been 'papered' with a Liberty lawn fabric mounted on iron-on vilene.

Two Edwardian Villas

The house shown opposite is an excellent starting point for a new dolls' house builder. It comes as a sturdy plywood kit with clear instructions from Honeychurch Toys. Jane and I decided to assemble one each, Jane's was to be influenced by Art Nouveau and she opted for a bathroom but left out the stairs. Mine was to have several Edwardian features like a high plate shelf round the room and greenery-yellery Arts and Crafts touches. I put in an upstairs parlour and a chilly blue bedroom and we both added a pretty verandah to the front, inspired by real houses of the Edwardian period in our neighbourhood. Mine was assembled first and, as a novice, I painted the brickwork freehand with oilpaints in a rather hit and miss fashion. However, the exterior of Jane's house is slightly more professional!

Jane laid the house fronts flat before gluing on any of the trim round the windows or door, and using a long metal ruler and a craft knife, scored all the horizontal lines of the exterior brickwork. Although this was tedious it was only done on the front, and the vertical lines were kept to a simple alternate brick bond. For the inside, she scored the floors in a similar way to simulate planks, and stained and varnished them before the house was assembled (see also page 109).

The brick guide-lines showed up most usefully through a thin wash of mortar-coloured water-based emulsion paint acting as an undercoat. Jane then had fun planning out the patterns of coloured bricks in pencil, taking her inspiration from a modest little house in Cardiff illustrated in a book about British domestic architecture. She used a beaten-up old flat brush that did not exceed the width of one brick to paint them in artist's oils.

The stained glass window above the front door (see left) was made by using the German 'Deka' brand glass paints. Trail out some of their contour paste for the outlines, following a design laid under the piece of perspex (plexiglass) or glass. You can then make puddles of rich colours within each enclosed area. The black outlines are a little coarse and wobbly for proper miniature scale, but the effect suited the chunky little house. New front doors were made by sandwiching a sheet of acetate between two thin layers of bass wood cut out to give us more stained glass panels.

The verandah was made by attaching 3 in (75 mm) wide strips of $\frac{1}{4}$ in (7 mm) wood to the opening fronts with wood glue and screws. The house then needed a couple of steps up to the front door (a little worn down in the middle). We drilled the floor and top bar to take the dowelling posts securely, and the perspex roof is supported by this and triangular pieces at the sides. The verandah railing is a ready-made, 8 in (200 mm) cheap, plastic moulding, and we snipped out a section to make glazing bars on the upper windows. The other scalloped plastic strip, sold for gable-trim, not only came in handy for the verandah but also reappears on the roof to resemble decorative ridge tiles combined with right-angled moulding from the timber yard. The roof was thickly painted in slate gray emulsion and scratched with a dead ball-point pen to look like tiles.

Of course, you can buy individual roof tiles, proper terracotta ridge tiles from potters in miniature, fancy posts turned on lathes and real metal 'wrought iron', but our methods were alternatives for novices on a budget.

Jane's ground floor sitting room, where the children are raiding a box of chocolates, is 'papered' with a fine Liberty lawn fabric backed with iron-on vilene fabric stiffener. Puce and lavender were deemed to be the most suitable period colours for the scheme. The other papers are conventional dolls' house ones except for the kitchen dado which is a particular section of a real-life embossed paper cut out and painted the most revolting Edwardian brown. The bedroom furniture is an unusual hand-carved Art Nouveau set by Miren Tong and the bathroom is splendiferous with its mahogany loo seat and authentic geyser.

My version of the house is known as The British Raj. The idea started with a couple of pressed metal tables that looked like carved Indian teak when painted brown, and then the theme ran away with me and suitable accessories kept presenting themselves. There is a David Edwards folding bamboo table, a wicker chair, an Indian hexagonal table and another I made by sticking a brass tray onto a souvenir wooden elephant. There is an Indian Benares brass log box and a spangly Indian cushion, a dear little ivory camel, a fly swatter, a ridiculous tiger skin rug and a wonderful procession of elephants marching along a tusk which I just knew would fit onto the mantelpiece shelf.

The miniaturized family photographs of a friend's grandfather and his polo pony and his incredibly numerous Indian household staff adorn the walls. Janice Crawley of Canada just happened to make an elephant tea set in celadon green – she appeared a little bemused on her first visit to England when one of her customers leapt up and down calling for her friend to 'Come and see the ducky little British Raj tea-pot, won't the Memsahib be pleased!'. A beaded purse depicting an elephant made an interesting wall hanging, and finally Colonel Blimp himself arrived complete with monocle and gouty foot swathed in bandages.

Time in this house seems to be a bit haywire as breakfast is being served in the kitchen, tea in the drawing room and dinner in the dining room. I'm obviously not as strong minded as a collector friend who has stacks of exquisite food hidden away in a large drawer and won't even put it in her dolls' house larder because they are all meant to be hot dishes!

A Victorian House

The shape of this American kit house (see overleaf) is unusual because it does not open from the back like most American dolls' houses, nor from the front like most British ones. It is a cross section of a house, with its side wall missing, designed to be hung on a real wall for easy viewing. Provided you can get a

*S*uitable accessories for the British Raj villa include an Indian table by Lilliput Miniatures, a fly swatter by David Edwards, an antique ivory camel, an elephant tea set and a photograph of the Colonel in his younger days with his polo pony.

*T*he British Raj version of the Edwardian villa is full of souvenirs of the Colonel's years in India. The Edwardian-looking ground floor carpet is a rectangle of velvet with an inset panel of a darker tone. The inexpensive sideboard had the cane on its doors replaced by the filigree ribs from a Chinese fan, and the printed leather screen is made from an old evening purse.

The contents of this house (*left*) are viewed through a permanently open side wall. The 'McKinley' house comes as a kit from Greenleaf in the USA and is shallow enough to be wall-hung which makes it an attractive showcase in your home.

Muriel Hopwood was inspired for these pieces by the Nanking porcelain dredged up from a long lost ship wreck. Ken Palmer made the silver top to the biscuit barrel.

sheet of perspex cut to shape to keep out the dust, it is attractive to be able to glance at the contents without having to stop to open up your dolls' house. It is one of the many kits made by the American firm of Greenleaf, and is readily available in Britain too.

These kits are made from fairly thin, coarse material that is only three-quarters pressed out of sheets. It can splinter away at the edges so be careful. The advantage of these kits is that they are very light and the glue, tab and slot assembly is designed to be easy for a beginner. The shapes in high Victorian style with turrets and porches are very pretty and not commonly available from British makers.

To make life easy, beg, borrow or steal a hot glue gun to assemble this kit, and expect to have to do a great deal of extra floor laying and pernickety roof tiling and weather boarding before the house looks as pretty as it does in the picture opposite. The edges of the floors that face outwards also look much neater now that they have been faced with thin strips of wood.

I would also advise doing a dummy run with as few spurts of glue as will keep the carcase together so that you can look at the shape and decide on any alterations of the layout before you've gone too far. Here, a separate landing has been replaced with a false door on the back wall of the upstairs sitting room. A study has been made where one might expect to have a bathroom.

There are many different interpretations of this house to be seen in American dolls' house magazines.

The Victorian period is probably the most popular with new collectors as there is a very wide selection of furniture available, particularly among the less costly ranges. There are also plenty of mini wallpapers to choose from. The cluttered style means that it doesn't matter if a dolls' house hasn't really got properly scaled rooms – one can happily crowd furniture together and carry on accessorizing it almost *ad infinitum*. Gas mantels, oil lamps and various light fittings of the Victorian era also come in the cheaper kit forms. This house was wired with flex (flexible insulated wire), not the copper tape system, and one of the drawers, disguised behind the fretwork at the base of the house, contains the connecting block and loops of slack wire.

In the dolls' house world, I have found people very willing to share good ideas and make 'one for you and one for me'. You will probably spot several twin items in this house – belonging to Jane – and my grandmamma's parlour (page 102). For instance, there is an inexpensive plaster fireplace which is painted in oils to look like 'vert antique' marble here and like 'rouge roi' marble in my parlour. Over both fireplaces hang remarkably similar shell-encrusted hand-bag mirrors. Jane modelled some brightly coloured fruit pretending to be Victorian wax fruit under a glass dome and I repaid the compliment with another dome that has the tiniest shells I could find wired into flowers. I used the copper strands out of life-size electric flex for the stems, planted into blobs of plasticine while the glue dried on the shells.

Over the years I have gradually progressed from using one small screw-driver as a substitute for a bradawl and/or a chisel. A mini drill, and an electric vibrating fret saw for curly Victoriana that turns the tightest corners but refuses to cut anything soft, so it leaves your finger tips intact, are also exceedingly useful. However, this house is eloquent testimony that the only essential tool for a budding collector and mini decorator is a neat little aluminium mitring block with a fine toothed saw made by X-acto for cutting the cornices into the corners.

A Victorian Mansion

Victorian is a term that tends to cover a multitude of sins in dolls' house styling. With the house pictured on pages 2 and 3, I originally intended to build a Georgian house because, like many a beginner, I thought I could manage flat fronts and uniform rectilinear windows. However, as my collecting years went by, I kept slipping further and further forward with wondrous gadgets like a mechanical mop-squeezing pail and a fine hot water geyser. My explanation is that a Victorian generation is living in an inherited Georgian house. They have put in a bathroom for the master bedroom but the servants still have to use an old 'thunder-box' loo. They have also modernized their lighting in fits and starts, which I confess has more to do with my evolution as a collector than any master plan.

One has to suspend disbelief so much anyway with a one room deep cabinet style of house that I adopted the unrealistic spirit of antique Baby Houses and built a conservatory with 'glass walls' and sloping roof which is actually inside a sky blue papered internal 'room' off the drawing room. I made the door panels out of thin dividers in cigar-boxes and used pressed timberyard mouldings for cornices. At that time, newly built dolls' houses as a hobby for adults were still a rarity and I hadn't yet made the right connections. By the time Jane built her big house (page 30) all the proper scale door kits and finely detailed mouldings were becoming more readily available. It is a real test of friendship when a latecomer's results far surpass your own.

In many ways then, this house is far from being an authentic representation of the Victorian era. The kitchen is in a bay-windowed reception room and the larder is next to the front hall which is all wrong. My house is out of scale, too, it is shallow from front to back because I was using a partly made shell. The advantage of this is that one doesn't knock so many things over as when reaching a hand into a very deep dolls' house room.

I had endless problems with the staircase in such a shallow hall. I left room for a token door opening into the rooms and then had to get the stairs to rise very steeply. The angles and kite-winders took ages to work out and then I forgot that once the house was at a comfortable height to view one would see the rough unfinished undersides of the treads. I hastily installed some arches which also conceal the fact that the dolls have to crawl past the turn for lack of

$\mathcal{A}$ bathroom can be just as rewarding to furnish as a grand drawing room if you take an interest in the date that safety razors with separate blades replaced the old 'cut throat' kind, and you hunt down the correct coal tar soap or cork bath mat.

headroom. I know building regulations require two spindles per tread in a stair-rail; but I only discovered packets of turned newel posts and banisters belatedly and installed them with mortal difficulty and a race against the hot glue gun. I think the finished effect is fine; I'm only confessing to all my shortcomings so that other novice builders can take heart.

I like having doll inhabitants doing things all over the place and kept acquiring more staff in an obvious case of wish fulfilment. My eldest son was very prone to scandalous re-arrangements of their activities, but I soon learnt the wisdom of a quick check before visitors were shown in. Do not waste anything you have the bad luck to break, you can always say Cook dropped it when she was frightened by a little ivory mouse.

There's one chap sitting in the very unusual Turkish bath by Bryntor Miniatures. He had to be specially ordered with a thin neck and pink feet as boots obviously wouldn't do. I had meant him to be the twin of the father

The study is full of trophies and travel mementoes. It radiates a cosy warmth because of careful ministering to Grandpa's creature comforts. He has a footstool, brandy and cigars to hand and a conveniently placed ash tray. The carpet was a lucky find of velour fabric printed in Persian designs and the chair seats are covered in rich soft silk from an old tie.

figure, thinking that I would swap them around between bath and library. When he turned out different I decided he had to be the legitimate master of the house if he was having all those long baths, so the other fellow was demoted. He's now the ne'er do well uncle sneaking up to the decanters in the dining room. He will soon be sent to The Colonies on a monthly remittance.

The study contains objects at all levels of collecting, from the most ordinary pencil sharpener globe in a corner up to a superb model ship with every minute piece of rigging present and correct. The books vary from genuinely printed miniature texts, through bindings from kits to home-made improvizations from magazine pictures. I had already used shells to frame a mirror and make flowers under a dome. Here there are some real small shells mounted for display on square black beads and tiny ones in a wall-hung case.

For the drawing room of this Georgian house, now 'inhabited' in the Victorian era, I cut panels from a gift wrap to look like early Chinese wallpaper and have used old embroidered silk as a carpet. This and other imperfections of scale convey the friendly feeling of an old dolls' house rather than the cool perfection of a model.

In the glass topped table are some cast metal pretend ones and there is a book about shells lying handy.

I went to visit the very famous 1730 dolls' house in a stately home called Uppark near Petersfield in Hampshire, England. It is indeed the most wonderfully preserved picture of Georgian life in miniature. It was there that I realized what strange large glass 'lids' with hangers were for. I mean, I had puzzled over some in full-size and then saw miniature versions in the dolls' house fulfilling their function of protecting the ceilings from candle smoke.

Visiting such stately homes can often inspire, and at Uppark I discovered the butler's pantry with a stone sink, fed by meandering lead pipes, that had an ingenious shelf over it with large holes through which one could support inverted decanters to drain – a brilliant contrivance that I promptly copied

for my dolls' house. It also inspired me to make a housekeeper's desk (page 130) with marble paper accounts books for staff wages, the cellar and the tradesmen. I wrote a cross letter to the butcher with a 0.13 draughtsman's pen. There are bills on a spike, bunches of keys and useful things like brown paper and string in a wooden dispenser and even green card luggage labels.

To marbleize small squares of paper for the books, fill a kitchen bowl with water and let a few finely scattered droplets of thin oil-based paint float on the surface. Gently stir to and fro with a pinhead to get some interesting swirls then lay a piece of paper, about 3 in (75 mm) square, flat onto the floating paint. Pick it up by one corner and a film of colour will adhere to the paper. You can do this several times with the same droplets of paint or after a tiny drop of another colour has been added and re-swirled around. Repeat until the paint no longer covers the paper. It is often not the first sheet that eventually looks the best.

Little pieces of this marble paper can be stuck over the front and back covers of plain, dark, inexpensive Taiwan books. Leave triangles of 'leather' showing at the opening corners for instant old fashioned accounts books. You will have plenty for covered boxes, desk sets, artists' portfolios, box files in an office, candle shades or whatever you have noticed made of marbleized paper in real life. You can of course dip other objects into the floating paint, such as a plain vase which will emerge looking swirly patterned like Art Deco glass.

In case you are confused by the word marbleized, let me explain that this sort of method, as in old book endpapers, does not produce the right sort of pattern to do duty as real stone marble. That is the 'faux marbre' or 'trompe l'oeil' so beloved of fashionable interior decorators. This effect is achieved by direct painting of blended splodges and streaks with fine veining added and I would advise always having a picture of real marble on hand to guide you.

A Georgian Mansion

Jane's big Georgian house is a very good example of an amateur builder achieving a high standard by using nicely detailed, bought components in the correct scale. She was able to achieve the spacious and gracious proportions she wanted by planning the shell herself in a manner that would be un-economic for most shops to stock as a ready-made house. Real rooms in rather grand eighteenth-century houses were often 15 ft (4.5 m) tall which is wildly extravagant by today's 8 ft (2.4 m) building norm. One can't begin to fit in six panel doors with pictures in over-door frames and then leave a gap before an

The Georgian mansion has an extra wide stair-well to allow room for furniture on the landings. The panelling has been continued onto the front opening façades of the house although this entails calculating gaps at the corners to permit the heavier cornices to swing back together.

elaborate dentil-moulded cornice if the basic height is not available in the dolls' house.

The floors were grooved, stained, 'nail holed' and varnished before assembly. As flex, not copper tape, was used for lighting, Jane made channels in the ceilings that could be conveniently filled in with ready-made sizes of wooden strips. This was also done with the plywood sheets laid flat before assembly. Tidy channels are formed by a router bit in the mini-drill held upright in a special frame. Alternatively, you can score the outlines of a channel several times with a craft knife held against a steel ruler and then gouge out the waste wood in the middle with a small screwdriver doing duty as a chisel.

The lighting consists only of candles which is authentic for the period (1820). Even oil lamps were not commonly in use till the middle of the nineteenth century. A dolls' house electrician increased the resistance on a transformer so that the usual 12-volt bulbs do not burn too brightly when they are seen as unshaded candles. You must not on any account meddle with the insides of a transformer yourself; indeed, those sold for 'toy' purposes are required to be permanently sealed.

Anyone decorating a front opening house has awkward decisions to make about how to treat the swing back fronts inside. If the room has heavy cornices, it ends up with odd looking gaps at the corners where allowances have been made for the mitres to swing back together when the façades are closed. Another problem is how to mark the thickness of the floors. Jane stuck strips of brown stained wood to demarcate the different decorative colour schemes and continued all her panelling onto the opening fronts. A quicker solution is to have a patchwork of wallpapers, as on my big house (pages 2–3). Yet another solution is to ignore the relationship between the rooms and the fronts and just paint or paper the same from top to bottom, as on the Gothic Castle (page 8).

The kitchen has 'stone' flags on the floor and 'bricks' behind the cooking range which are bought as components from Sussex Crafts and Terry Curran. The wainscot panelling is made with $\frac{1}{16}$ in (2 mm), obeche strips, a typically neutral fine grain wood like bass which is commonly available. First cut enough pieces, with the grain running upright, to fit round the room, then scratch it with a sharp metal point to look like tongue and groove panelling and let a generous application of stain soak into the grooves. Light oak stain on raw wood gives an attractive, mature pine look, but don't be afraid to experiment – dolls' house decorators can take liberties.

The sink in the corner has a water pump, taps would be out of period. Notice also that the saucepans have still got the early flat lids with long handles. They are hanging on home-made shelves with neat little hooks that Jane made by slightly opening a commercially available small brass eye. There is a traditional spice cupboard with lots of little drawers that precedes

$\mathcal{R}$esearching and portraying domestic implements of a bygone age provide endless fascination in the miniatures hobby. This kitchen has a meat hastener in front of the range: a joint of meat used to be cooked in front of the open fire by revolving the suspended meat inside the semi-circular copper shield.

more modern spice jars. The spices would then have to be pounded in a mortar and pestle by the cook.

In the drawing room seen on the left of page 30 there is a rather grandly framed painting over the drawing room fireplace. This is in fact an art gallery's advertisement framed with four corner elements from an excellent range of plastic curlicues called Shortwood Carvings. Do be careful to date your paintings to match your furnishings, you can get as ancestral as you like in portraits but you cannot have the lady in the painting wearing a later fashion than the dolls' house inhabitant. Jane dressed the dolls in high waisted Regency styles but the little blackamoor page boy was a special order from Sunday Dolls.

The music room (overleaf) is dominated by a framed wall hanging taken from a sheet of wrapping paper. The sofa and the wing chair come from Real Life kits that have good early lines. The yellow silk used on the chair was taken

This library also serves as a music room. Although there are not many pieces of furniture, and certainly none the owner would wish to eliminate, it is difficult to give dolls' houses the spaciousness of a real stately home of the Georgian period.

from an old book binding. Jane did some real book binding when she found a gift-wrap that had Ye Olde looking botanical prints in small squares. She cut out prints and mounted them on vellum paper, stitching them together into covers made of card covered in book-end marble paper with leather-look paper for triangular corners and the spine.

The other books on the shelves are mostly the kind that come as a nicely printed sheet of bindings and appropriately marked out card to cut into a stack of 'pages' to fill them. We have also made good looking books by keeping our beady eyes open for advertisements for traditionally bound encyclopaedia sets. The spines of simple books or ones mocked up out of gilt edged balsa blocks can easily be improved by sticking the advertisements over the top. I do wish book, clock, record and Christmas card advertisers would kindly take their pictures head on and not intrude their messages on the items I want to cut out!

The handsome bookshelves were made to measure to fit either side of the chimney breast. It's not difficult to get a very neat finish by using fine strips of bought double beading to face the shelf edges. When you look at real old furniture and fittings it is amazing what elaborate care was lavished even on kitchen pieces. A dolls' house decorator can do a great deal to improve home-made items with extra mouldings or by laying a better shaped top over an inexpensive piece of furniture or a mantelpiece. The fireplace here was a kit that received the 'add on a few bits and see what it looks like all painted over' treatment. The mirror frame is one of the extensive range of frames and good architectural components made by Unique Miniatures in the USA.

The other furniture in the music room is by good miniature craftsmen such as Barry Norbury for the Regency chairs, John Otway for the spinet and Roger Gutheil for the reading stand with candle holders. There is an in-expensive white metal cast chess set from Phoenix models which has been upgraded by standing it on a nicely inlaid wooden board. The trumpet comes from the British Museum gift shop, the recorder from Wentways Miniatures, the lute is exquisitely made by Jim Whitehouse and the harp is home-made from a superior do-it-yourself pattern by Virginia Merrill.

The Chinese bedroom (see page 122) in this Georgian house is a nod towards the ebullient Chinese designs of John Nash's interiors for the Prince Regent's Brighton Pavilion, begun in 1815. Chinese wallpapers were the first to be used in England and were prized imports all through the eighteenth century.

Two Second-hand Homes

When does a battered hand-me-down dolls' house become a valuable antique? Is it all right to re-furbish an old house, and if so, how far should one go? These are very difficult questions to answer in the dolls' house field. There is a lot to be said for starting as a miniaturist in a second-hand home, just as young couples learn new skills in their homesteading years of stripping and refurbishing junk furniture.

If you acquire a second hand dolls' house in a car boot sale it is not very likely that it will be a priceless heirloom, but for peace of mind: check it out. Look for a label, a number or a symbol; not forgetting to search the underside of the base and inside the roof if it lifts off. Unfortunately, style is nothing to go by, a 'Tudor' house is more likely to have rolled out of the Triang factory in the 1950s than to have been built by Henry VIII's carpenter.

Take a photograph of it or sketch it, write down its dimensions and send this information with a stamped addressed envelope to someone qualified to advise

$\mathcal{S}$ea View (*above*) is proof that no matter how simple your dolls' house, you can derive enormous enjoyment from following through a particular theme. I did just that here in collecting all manner of nautical souvenirs and in doing an affectionate send-up of the inhabitants' taste in kitsch.

you. When you have established what you now own, you can think about what the house might have looked like in its prime and gently coax it back to life. Study books about old dolls' houses or visit museums that have them on show and see what you can find, make or 'doctor' to furnish your house sympathetically.

If you don't really have a natural feel for older houses and you'd rather feel free to do your own thing with nice shiny new paint, then, personally, I would beg you to give the old dolls' house you are contemplating 'doing up' to a good home and start with a nice clean plywood shell.

The two old houses featured here illustrate the difference between an antique with a known provenance, like the timbered cottage made by Lines in about 1922, which I have filled myself but left materially untouched, and the jokey seaside bungalow which was untraceable and had no original papers.

As old dolls' houses were often papered in full-size wallpaper I think it's nice to look among these and gift wraps rather than the perfect scale miniature prints. Avoid white background colours, go for a softer, murkier look or try spongeing them with tea or coffee. You will quickly realise that refined perfect miniature furniture looks all wrong. The good news is that it's the cheaper, clumsier imports or amateurishly made pieces that will look more at home in a

On the left of the picture on the *previous page* is Sea View, my much loved 'horrible' bungalow. I felt free to embellish it with a mermaid in a new front garden because the house could not be traced to a known maker. The worn roof paper has deliberately been left in its original state, however, as the patina of wear and tear will increase the value of the dolls' house as we grow antique together.

The cottage on the right appears in a 1922 catalogue of Lines Brothers' houses and has been kept 'unimproved'.

dolls' house that has probably got some clumsy features of its own like a crude fireplace or plain slabs for doors. These pieces start looking quite at home, when rubbed down with wire wool to take off the new gloss or re-upholstered in a more suitable scrap of old fabric.

It was love at first sight between Sea View and me. I had spent years immersed in the eighteenth and nineteenth centuries for my big mansion and I just stood and laughed at this daft looking little bungalow with its comic top knot of a chimney. The awful ordinariness of the pebble dash and green paint was quite enchanting, and what clinched the sale was that the dealer had hung some 'horrible' purple flowered curtains best side out... It just had to be a pre-war seaside residence.

I sailed through decorating it on a honeymoon cloud of love and giggles. Sea gulls landed on its roof via souvenir ash-trays, a mermaid washed up and found herself the ideal piece of Cornish slate to lie on. I had an assortment of shells to hand, plastic lilies of the valley converted in a trice to hollyhocks and there were the 'silver bells and cockle shells and pretty maids all in a row' from the nursery rhyme Mary, Mary, Quite Contrary. I appropriated a model boat and used a scrap of crumpled green hat veiling for a fishing net. A sea horse button turned up for the doorknocker and a junk model dog repainted black and tan became Rover for the doorstep. Barnacle Bill, hurricane lamp jewellery pendant, picnic hamper, nautical flags, coils of rope – it was hard to stem the flood.

What has been such added fun is the participation of dolls' house friends. Sea View obviously touched a chord and I have been generously showered with ship-embossed brass plates, flying ducks for the wall, a lighthouse lamp, a ship in a bottle and a scrimshaw whale's tooth, cake decoration swimming belle statuettes, an old 'smoker's set', the perfect fan-shaped triple mirror, and even a knitted bathing suit.

Inside I used a full-size shell-shaped Laura Ashley paper which looked very 1930s. In the other room there is a striped dolls' house paper juxtaposed with a lurid bottle green dado and picture rail. The paint work is the ever popular 'Magnolia' shade of cream. I left the old parquet effect paper on the floor and added some pretty nasty bits of patterned carpet and a rush door mat.

The furnishings are a mixture of new things doctored down and old dolls' house toys, like the overscale but 'working' sewing machine, the cooker and the refrigerator (bit of a luxury for a bungalow?). I bought a shiny Taiwan gate-leg table and ruthlessly attacked it with paint stripper, whereupon it promptly fell to pieces. I scrubbed the components and glued them back together and now it goes perfectly with the cheap and cheerful chairs that I also attacked with coarse sandpaper.

The typical patent kitchen cabinet with the drop down shelf was inspired by a neat cream and red enamel bread bin. I painted two plastic pieces extended in the middle to take a mock up of the shelf and stuck halves of metal press

The wallpapers in the miner's cottage are original as is the rather crude-looking, brick papered fireplace upstairs. The furniture is old, in the 1/16th scale, which is why the longjohns and the boots look so big. They were too endearing not to use and old dolls' houses seem to accommodate variations in scale quite happily. The miner is being attended by a doll home-made in my childhood.

studs on the lower doors to represent the ventilation gadgets. The ironing board was 'singed' with dilute brown stain and I wrapped a hairy piece of old silk-covered dolls' house lamp flex round a model iron. I suspect that they plug it in to the central light with one of those perilous old socket converters.

Sea View had a hole in the back of its roof and some vestiges of battery lighting so I deliberately used torch bulbs for its central hanging lamps to keep to the right look. However, I did have to use mini bulbs to poke into the 'electric' heater and the lighthouse lamp. One lampshade was an incredibly lucky find with its wonderful orange camels and pyramids and green palm trees. The other is made of curtain rings and a pleated marble-patterned paper which looks like parchment. There is also a real parchment shade, made with the authentic whipping stitches, with red toadstools (could one ask for more?) that came on a lamp from my childhood dolls' house.

The inhabitants, Mr and Mrs Everyman, are dolls that I had from my childhood, too, but as dolls' house fashions often lagged well behind real-life I think they look quite prissy and short-back-and-sides enough to pass for a good decade earlier. Young Christopher came rather late in their lives and I hope you notice his baggy gray shorts and grubby sweater. His socks are made from a tiny piece of old vest glued round his ankles. He is holding a jar of tadpoles and frowning because he wants to get back down to the beach, not hang about with cousin Vera, a boring girl.

The little Lines cottage is too small for 1/12th-scale furniture although there are accessories that seem to cross scale borders quite happily in this sort of imperfect setting. The house had an enormous tin stove with a printed cardboard back that said 'Dolly's Kitchen Range'. However, it was impossible to fit in even small 1/16th-scale furniture beside it, so after much heart-searching I replaced it with a better 'model' of an old fashioned range and mantelpiece, but I have carefully kept the original for posterity.

A friend gave me a wonderful pair of longjohns made out of a soft and creamy old vest complete with a little trap door opening at the back. They started me off on the DH Lawrence miner's cottage theme which I continued with those little cards of pious mottoes.

The miner is sitting in the tub, made by Colin Roberson. The first time he was made, I complained that he wasn't sufficiently immersed in his suds. Not for reasons of modesty, but because he didn't quite look as if he was sitting on the floor of the tub and it is important to get such details right. However, he is being looked after by a hopelessly unrealistic female doll, but then I made her myself when I was twelve, and one should be loyal to one's old friends.

Your Own Home

There are many reasons why you might like to recreate your own home or a particular house in miniature. You may have vivid memories of a childhood home, or a house that you once lived in which would act as a starting point.

The 'Linley Sambourne' house (see pages 63–7), for example, shows the value of consulting a prime example of a style in real life when attempting a Victorian setting. For reference material constantly to hand, you can't beat making a model of your own home, which can be tremendous fun. However, it will inevitably mean making many items from scratch, or some compromises if that is beyond your skill.

Miniatures tend to lag behind modern design, especially in fitted kitchens. In the States, there is far more contemporary furniture available than in Europe, where plexiglass coffee tables, angular chairs and shower cubicles are more likely to be found in the Lundby 1/16th-scale, mass-produced dolls' house furniture than in the craftsmen's ranges. You will, of course, have no major problems if your real house is mainly furnished with antiques and has a fashionably nostalgic Edwardian bathroom.

The house shown here is the home of Pam Cornish, an extremely enterprising and ingenious maker as well as a long-standing collector. She began the model

This photograph of the real home of Pam and Bryan Cornish demonstrates how faithfully Pam modelled the house in 1/12th scale. This kind of model needs ingenious opening arrangements, like the side panel which lifts away between the two outbuildings.

of her own two-hundred-year-old cottage by working from full-size architect's plans. Those were the pioneering days of the adult hobby in Britain, so she had to contrive her own weatherboarding by cutting sheets of hardboard into innumerable strips. She used dowelling and half rounds for drainpipes and gutters and achieved realistic slates by painting hundreds of card price-tags in slight variations of gray before glueing them onto the roof.

The real cottage is basically one room deep by three rooms wide, so she made two end walls that open on hinges and two side panels that lift away to give access to the middle room and the stairs. It also has various small extensions to house modern plumbing, which necessitated lift-off roofs and the most fearsome complications in the way of electric wiring. There are four sets of separately controlled lights whose wires terminate in switches neatly concealed outside the building by a hollow-bottomed tub of flowers.

Pam made her own copies of her full-size dining table and chairs as well as the old pine dresser. The real one holds her collection of blue and white Staffordshire pottery and the miniature one has lovely hand-painted willow pattern plates and as many similar items as she could find. These are mostly by Rosamund Henley, a marvellous miniature artist who saddened us all by returning to a 'big' job some years ago.

The kitchen and bathroom are all faithful to the real thing. Luckily, the real kitchen cupboards had louvre doors which could be made from dolls' house shutters. There are a few special pieces of furniture which were commissioned in miniature, but many others were contrived from a kit or an inexpensive piece as a starting point. Family photos and framed black crayon rubbings of old tombstone brasses are reduced versions of those originally made by the owner before dolls' houses swallowed up all her creative hours.

A Thatched Cottage

In furnishing a dolls' house built to a period style it is important to decide how the contents are to be dated. You can travel in time through a couple of centuries of additions and alterations right up to Kleenex tissues and Ketchup bottles, but if you have given the house some inhabitants, the decorative style must stop at the date to which they are dressed. In the case of this little thatched cottage made by Hollycraft, I spent ages wondering whether it was a cute country retreat with all mod cons or what? The poor thing sat there looking forlorn till I came across a pre-war book called *Old English Household Life* and found the answer: the outside looked seventeenth century, so I could furnish the inside to match. The book's illustrations provided me with a ready-made shopping list for furniture and fittings.

Over the next year I found a lovely oak monk's table from Wentways – this is a chair whose back folds down to rest on the arms and form a table. Wentways also make a good joint stool. An Escutcheon gate-leg table was just right but the matching dark oak chairs came upholstered in wine red leather which seemed too sophisticated for my purpose, so I took a deep breath and painted them with shoe dye. A rather clumsy pine settle was darkened with stain and touches of paint where the stain wouldn't take on the glue. My accomplice Jane said I was fully justified in spending rather a lot of money on a lovely antique miniature dower chest, 'Made for it', she said, 'You were meant to have it', so I bought it with a perfectly clear conscience.

Various simple black firebaskets, three-legged pots, trivets and kettle hangers came from Terry McAlister, who read my pre-war book from cover to

The exterior of the thatched cottage made in the style of a 1750s' house by Hollycraft. The entire roof tips up and back for access to the bedrooms. This then allows the ground floor façade to swing open. The open house can be seen on pages 18 and 19.

cover. He also made a basic turnspit to stand in front of the fire. I modelled a carcase to roast on it, complete with a puddle of varnish and paint in the drip-pan below.

There is a pile of sheep's wool on the floor next to a simple spinning wheel and a delicate yarn winder from Alan Waters of Australia which spins so entrancingly that I do not want to be told if it is too late for the period. The pewter mugs and dishes and the juicy haunch of venison on the table are definitely in period, however. I stuck to apples as I didn't think a cottager could have afforded exotic imported oranges. There isn't an oven so the loaf of bread is round and unleavened. I think the old boy in his shepherd's smock sitting by the fire could have acquired the brace of pheasants legitimately, as wild game was plentiful. The birds are wondrously made with real pheasant feathers by Rohanna Bryan, who also made the basket of scallop shells.

When one starts enumerating all the food like this it's obviously far too much for a simple peasant household who would be more likely to have to make do with a barley and root vegetable stew.

Hollycraft buried some electric flex in the fireplaces and here and there in the walls while the house was being built, as I'm very keen on bringing an interior to life with lights, providing they look appropriate. To light up, the rush-light holders would have needed fibre optics to be in scale, so I experimented with candlesticks. There are some very fine white plastic candle bodies with flame shaped bi-pin bulbs available from the USA, but they look too smooth for tallow candles. Eventually I hit upon the idea of rolling raw translucent Fimo modelling paste directly round the flex of grain of rice bulbs. (Fimo should be baked after modelling – it is obviously raw in this case.) It works very well because you can bring the Fimo a little way up the bulb and the light glows through the top of the candle most realistically.

I fiddled about with two curtain rings and a metal belt eyelet to make the equivalent of an old wrought iron hanging candle holder. The split flexes are stuck left and right in a figure of eight up the back of the rings. For some wall lights I took a short cut and merely removed the top of mass-produced plastic coach lamps to be left with rather good looking 'wrought iron' brackets.

The fires were no problem with concealed bulbs under orange tissue paper with twig 'logs' glued over them. I didn't use flickering fires here because I had no way of separating out the flex of the fires from the rest for the small electronic circuit board flicker units which interrupt the current along the route back to the transformer. There are now other flickering units that sit in the fireplace itself, but at the time the only ones available were either horribly expensive or seemed to blink out morse code messages rather than dancing firelight. I think a steady glow is quite acceptable.

Short of drilling holes in rather precious table tops there is frequently no way you can get a light where you want it without the problem of ugly flexes. I don't mind hooking flex through a carpet to conceal a run to the nearest wall but in the cottage there wasn't even a mat. I painted the flexes black and then stuck the lights on the table and reading chair with a little blob of gripwax. The flex was tied to the back of the furniture legs with matching sewing cotton. I smeared some more wax on the flex and took the most discreet line possible to a wall outlet.

All too frequently it is necessary to work backwards with lights instead of having all the positions worked out in advance and catered for with concealed wires or copper tape. I don't think one should worry about this at all, as a lot can be done to deceive the eye. It is important to disguise the wires, as it is so irritating to see a wavy white plastic flex trailing away from a so-called candle or oil lamp in an otherwise carefully executed miniature setting.

A Mobile Home

I spotted this extraordinary model of a mobile home in a shop window and bought it on impulse because a beloved aunt had ended her retirement days in a trailer park. I joyfully recognized each detail of its careful internal planning – the hatch between the kitchen and living room, the wealth of built-in fitments, the space-saving shower cubicle and even the neat little broom cupboard. The layout was identical to Aunty Peggy's and even the rather dated looking 1970s' orange tiling was just right.

The trailer is incredibly solidly built. All the room and cupboard door hinges are bolted through the doors with little brass nuts and meticulously filed down bolts. This may not be correct for the art of miniatures, and indeed I personally would never have picked the oversized bench cover fabric which absolutely does not go with the checked curtains, but the whole model has an integrity of careful observation and painstaking execution that I find very touching.

Although the bought shower and cloakroom fittings are in the commercial 1/16th scale not the 1/12th used elsewhere, the attention to detail is marvellous, right down to the door-stops in the bedrooms to stop the doors swinging back against the wonderful built-in dressing tables with stools to match and the strips of red carpet running carefully down the middle of the floor and finishing in a gray rubber doormat.

Funny accessories seem to make autonomous decisions to move in to this sort of dolls' house. This was the obvious home for a set of orange-lidded saucepans and a box of tea bags that was too modern for previous settings. Ready-cut strips of quilling paper made a good fly-catcher door curtain. A Spanish dancer and 'poron' wine jug are naturally souvenirs of a package holiday. I don't think it matters at all that the clockwork food processor is rather too big and that the TV set, which has click-round tourist views, is bright green plastic – it's the thought that counts.

The outside, too, is proper with removable steps up to the two glazed doors. There are wheels under the middle and two sets of splayed legs that actually fold away on a spring when it's time to hook up the towing gadget and move away. It stands on a piece of greengrocer's fake grass mat that serves quite well until the day I attempt serious landscaping around it. So far there are some patio furniture pieces, a garbage bin, two garden gnomes and a temporary infestation of mice and rabbits that had no other home.

On the *previous page*, in all its glory, is the unusual and endearing Mobile Home. The fabrics would not have been a true miniaturist's first choice but the work is too lovingly done for me to think of discarding it.

An Art Deco House

This was originally a four roomed house with a nondescript façade that was completely transformed and extended on either side with the help of an invaluable dolls' house handy-man. Barbara, the owner, decided that its date should be 1935, so the main features of the new, flat, white 'modern' front are curved windows with horizontal rectangles of metal glazing bars, a glazed 'sunburst' front door with a simple semi-circle porch roof and a typical 1930s' round stained-glass window of a ship in full sail. The flat roof was given a railing specially made to repeat the sunburst design. This is also repeated in the glass of the garage doors, made from planks laid in a chevron pattern.

The fruits of careful research and a real feeling for the period are immediately apparent inside the house. The stairs have boxed in bannisters and the internal doors are flat with handles two thirds of the way up. The rear windows with box pelmets emphasize the horizontal glazing bars and cream gloss paint is used throughout. As a finishing touch, railway panorama scenery paper featuring houses of the same period was mounted to be seen through these windows.

In the sitting room, which the proud owners doubtless called 'The Lounge', the walls are papered up to a picture rail with a beige moiré pattern. Below this rail runs a geometrical frieze in orange, green, black and gold, coloured and cut out by hand. The curtains are a suitably beige shade of shiny satin and the carpet was cut from plain beige dolls' house carpeting which was then transformed with a painted geometric pattern. There is, of course, a semi-circular brown hearth-rug in front of the boxy tiled fireplace with a stepped outline. This fireplace and the pink and black version next door were made from the mottled DIY mosaic tiling very popular in the 1950s. The central light was ingeniously made from two bought wall brackets from the USA that match the terrific triple standard lamp with trumpet lily shaped glass shades.

The semi-circular blond maple tub chairs with black bases and the truly wonderful sofa built into an arrangement of asymmetrical shelves and curved end cupboards were copied by Doug Woodyard from a 1928 picture of furniture by Englinger shown in *Mobilier et Décoration*. There is also a maple and ebony fold-down desk from the same designer. All the upholstery and scatter cushions had to be rigidly over-stuffed. The inhabitants of this house don't read many books but they listen to 'the wireless' somewhat obsessively as there are three very 1930s' looking radios in various rooms. There had to be a mirror-lined cocktail cabinet with a curved front and a chrome smoker's side table to complete the scene.

The accessories are a mixture of conversions and good finds. The wall ornaments came from a belt buckle and from a tulip brooch. The green dancer figure started life as a silver cake decoration, the running deer as charms from a bracelet. There is a milky glass 'Lalique' vase and another filled with the popular white calla lilies. The globe lamp with the little mermaid was made to look even more Deco with the addition of a round mirror behind it.

The dining room has a fashionably Oriental theme with pink dragon wallpaper and cane blinds which were cut from a table mat. The pink and black fireplace is very striking and the carpet was painted in a design of Vs in pink, green and brown. The light fitting was specially made with gold

The Art Deco house is typical of the 'modern' architecture popular in the western suburbs of London between the wars. The owner and her builder drove round gathering information for the characteristic features.

 $\mathscr{N}$othing could be more faithful to the interior design of the 1930s than this sitting room (*above*). The essential cocktail cabinet is seen closed on the left.

 $\mathscr{T}$he four rooms *opposite* are the dining room, kitchen, child's bedroom and bathroom of the Art Deco house. As furniture of this period is not readily available in miniature, the important pieces of furniture were commissioned.

coloured glass shades. The furniture was commissioned from Doug Woodyard, with a hexagonal table and chairs taken from a 1924 design by Groult. The originals had panels of stained tortoiseshell. The table is set with fine Art Deco china with its triangular handles. By strange coincidence, the porcelain artist June Astbury who made the miniature is the daughter of the original designer.

 The kitchen is painted in pale green, of course, and has a zinc enamel top table and a patent kitchen cabinet. The deep china butler's sink has a splashback of suitably rectangular white glazed tiles and there is an early manually operated washing machine from Bryntor Miniatures, a round-cornered re-

The great hall of the Scottish baronial castle was laboriously panelled throughout using lengths of grooved cross bars and pre-cut infill panels. The fireplace came as a complex kit and was then further ornamented with strips of pierced brass in the arches. The Irish wolf hound is a handsome beast that came from 'The Singing Tree', but he is not hairy like the wonderful stag trophy which can be seen in the picture of the ceiling details on page 117.

frigerator and a larder cupboard in the corner. Janice Crawley's tomato tea set is waiting to go onto the sunburst tray. The mass-produced set of saucepans have been painted by Barbara to look like cream and green enamel. The basic green and white floor paper was patiently ruled and shaded into double the number of small squares.

The same treatment was used for the floor of the blue bathroom which is behind the round stained glass window by Wentways. The bath had a 'transatlantic' style panel, but the real success of the room lies in the clever boxing in of all the fittings with layered Deco motifs added wherever possible. One wall has smoky gray mirrored tiling used horizontally to make stepped cupboards with an array of glass bottles and cosmetic jars by Hudson River.

The bedrooms are furnished with carefully chosen bought pieces and some extra ones made to match. A round shouldered wardrobe is old but the typical shell back chairs are available from the Taiwan ranges. There is an alabaster bowl lampshade in the main bedroom and a good period gas fire as well as more handpainted carpets. The child's bedroom has shell pattern wallpaper stuck on in panels with corner designs. The boxy-looking laundry basket and accessories like a wooden pencil box with a sliding lid and little figures of Mickey and Minnie Mouse add finishing touches. There is a picture of 'Lillibet', as Queen Elizabeth was known as a child, and she shares the honours with Shirley Temple who appears both in a photograph and as a doll.

A Gothic Castle

Early dolls' houses did not always have naturalistic exteriors and there is also something reminiscent of an old house's chunkiness about this one. Polished hardwoods and a strong sense of style are the speciality of its builder Samuel Halfpenny (exterior on page 8). It could sit in your living room and no one would dare to presume it had strayed out of the nursery. A previous house had attracted Jane and Samuel Halfpenny liked her commission so they got down to detailed plans very happily. It couldn't be too big, so forget all the other rooms which are somewhere 'round the back', but it absolutely had to have a tower and a chapel was felt to be essential.

The Castle, known as Rowan Lodge, is decorated in the fullblooded 'muscular Gothic' style of Augustus Pugin, decorator of the Palace of Westminster. AWN Pugin, one of the leaders of the nineteenth-century Gothic Revival, abhorred anything pretty and pastel; he stained his oak beams dark to look ancient and filled in every inch of ceiling space between them with brilliant pattern and colour. No half measures called for; where it wouldn't be panelled it would all have to be scarlet and bright blue and stained glass and gold. Baronial, you might say.

Baronial set us thinking: suits of armour, gruesome weapons, trophies, dead animals and things made out of parts thereof, like those ghastly deers' foot candlesticks and antler chairs in grim Scottish castles. A Scottish laird, Lord

The upstairs parlour of Rowan Lodge shows the dado panelling which has innumerable mitred squares, each containing a cut out trefoil beneath the crenelations. The arched cornice was fortunately available in a pre-cut wooden strip in the USA as it corresponded exactly to the cornice seen in the period reference pictures that inspired the theme for this 1/12th-scale room.

Dreerie of Weird, and his lady would have to live there, and they could have a daughter called Flora so that there was an excuse to have some toys to relieve the gloom. There ought to be a son and heir, so that is Alexander, known as Sandy, on account of his red hair and freckles.

Sunday Dolls turned up trumps on the inhabitants, but the furniture was more difficult to find. In the dolls' house world Victorian was synonymous with curvaceous lines and overstuffed upholstery, not right at all. By the greatest good fortune, Jane met a craftsman experienced in model boat building and marquetry. Perhaps he could help? The very first piece he produced was a masterpiece: it was the beautiful boxwood prie-Dieu for the chapel (page 112).

The tower has very little floor space and even less wall surface, so a free-standing prie-Dieu and a vase of tall white lilies as seen in so many of Rossetti's religious paintings just about fill it. My contribution was to do terrible things to a brass candelabra to convert it to a hanging light with pierced brass strips and an ecclesiastical dark red rope. It started out with wax candles but it was later electrified, once we had discovered really fine candle bodies and replaceable bi-pin bulbs from the USA.

Jane excelled herself at colouring and gilding plastic mouldings and adding brass motifs and trumpeting angels to every nook and cranny. The pillars are covered in a remarkably labour-saving gift wrap paper of dark blue with gold fleurs de lys. A similar red paper was used for the pillars in the entrance hall below, which naturally has an elephant foot umbrella stand. The stained glass window is a Pugin design photocopied onto clear plastic and coloured by hand.

The panelling in the baronial hall on the ground floor was also all done by hand. Borcraft Mouldings supply kits and detailed instructions for this and the triple arched fireplace. However, it was still extremely difficult to work out all the measurements and very confusing to visualize in which plane to cut all the beastly little mitred joins.

Finding statuettes for the arched niches and deciding on a motto to run along the fireplace was the fun part – *Nisi Dominus Frustra* which puts in a Latin nutshell the very apt sentiment: Unless the Lord builds the house the labour is in vain. Panelling upstairs was made much easier by using very fine plywood that could be cut with scissors into the crenellated shapes. The design for this and the arched cornice came from a picture of an 1857 princely hunting lodge in *Authentic Decor* by Peter Thornton.

Hanging in pride of place is a magnificent painting of 'The Monarch of the Glen'. It was re-created down to the last hair of the stag in the Landseer original and was the first commission for Judith Drury, an incomparable artist in the miniatures world. All the main pieces of furniture in the house are either based on Pugin originals, like the leather chairs designed for Carisbrook Castle, or his contemporaries' designs, like the complex roll-top desk adapted

from a design by Seddon. The leather upholstery, made by Jane, was done with the aid of an electric mini drill – invaluable help with the numerous rows of tiny holes for brass nails. Another usage no one ever seems to mention is how convenient it is to poke into a fully furnished dolls' house room with the flexible shaft and drill a little hole to take a minute nail for a picture. Please note that 'The Monarch' is hanging on chains as befits a weighty work of art.

The baronial theme was pursued through a wondrous antler chair, an Irish wolf-hound before the fire and a terrific stag head trophy made of real fur. The American artisan kindly explained that she uses white ermine fur so that she can dye it to the right colour and leave markings light, should that be appropriate to the beast. If you are too 'green' to use fur, you can manage an inferior substitute by beheading plastic toy zoo animals and mounting them on little shields of wood.

There is nothing squeamish about this household though, a glance in the kitchen will discover a hairy hare and a brace of feathery pheasants and a very dead fowl about to slither off the butcher's block. Because baronial kitchens were usually miles of freezing corridor away from the dining hall, you will find a good selection of food covers hanging ready on the wall. Old kitchens were most frequently painted in this shade of blue because the arsenic contained in blue paint helped to ward off the flies. This is another example of the scraps of general knowledge a dolls' house enthusiast acquires.

Two Charity Cottages

These charity cottages, known as almshouses in Britain, were usually a row of modest cottages built by a charity for the poor of the parish or by a benevolent landlord for retired tenant workers. In this latter case they were often executed in the style that matched other buildings on the estate.

This little house was built in the Victorian Gothic style as a one-off exercise by Kevin Mulvany. The delightful mellow exterior was achieved by coating the plywood with a smooth skim of plaster which was painted in cloudy patches of brick colour. The outlines of the bricks were carefully scored in the one long one short Flemish bond and the dress bricks, that make the patterns so beloved of even modest Victorian builders, were neatly overpainted. I added shading to the stone work round the windows to make the sills and reveals look deeper.

The inside was completely blank. The four rooms had been treated as belonging to the same house and there was only one staircase, but I didn't like the idea of a weekend conversion, so I reverted to the two separate establishments that corresponded to the façade. This meant that one household would be oddly stairless, but the thought of cutting my way through the floor of a finished house seemed too daunting, so I opted for the powers of suggestion.

Out came the kitchen scissors and various pieces of cereal carton were offered up to devise a little rear lobby and a filled-in triangle representing the

This is the more prosperous Mrs Jones' side of the semi-detached charity cottages (you can also see her curtains in the chapter on soft furnishings on page 138). The clotted cream colour of the plastered walls was very popular in English cottages and the idea of having a cut out floral paper border also came from a real house.

Mrs Smith's cottage shows how an inglenook fireplace was created next to the unusual forward-facing slope under the stairs. The 'Orkney' chair with a woven rope back is made by Rudeigin Beag from an old Scottish design.

Mrs Smith has shoe polish and cough mixture among the articles on the mantelpiece and some of her pictures are torn out of magazines. Her dresser carries more earthenware and simpler pottery plates than her neighbour's. The traditionally framed motto above her bed shows a beehive and reads 'Be not slothful'.

underside of a staircase that one can imagine surfacing behind the wall of the room above. The angles were looking very steep, even for cottage stairs, so I pushed the fake door as far as possible across the bedroom and cut off the corner of the doorframe against the slope of the ceiling in a thoroughly cottagey fashion. I ran out of the house at midnight to look at the 'Suffolk latch' on our back gate by torchlight and managed to make a passable copy of it with soft lead from the neck of a wine bottle.

Once the layout was finalized and the cardboard mock-ups converted to more solid plywood, it was time to give the inside more character. I covered the walls with rough plaster made of glue and filling compound mixture, laid on with the tool sold for artists' oil paints which proved just right for a dolls' house plasterer's trowel. The lines of the pointy pitched ceilings were highlighted with belated beams faked up with strips of wood veneer. More compound mixture was used to make slate-flagged floors downstairs.

A book about English cottages contained a photograph of an elderly couple at their primitive open hearth, with firedogs to hold up the logs, which seemed unchanged for centuries. In another picture I suddenly realized that there was a photograph of Queen Elizabeth II in a very old-fashioned looking setting where oil lamps were still in use. By filling in part of the triangular space under the stairs, I created an inglenook wide enough to take a windsor chair for one house, and the other ran to a nicely blacked kitchen range with plenty of gleaming horse brasses.

So the idea of two elderly ladies, Mrs Smith and Mrs Jones, was born. They would still call each other Mrs even though they had been neighbours for years. Of course Mrs Smith wouldn't quite be able to keep up with Mrs Jones who had got 'the electric', as she would say, and was generally just that bit more prosperous. Incidentally, Mrs Jones has got a little brown window envelope with the electricity bill on her mantelpiece.

I studied more photographs and checked off a long list of Staffordshire china dogs, simple mantel clocks, jar of spills, bellows, warming pan, stone hot water bottle, jug with little net cover weighted with beads, calendars and photographs of Royalty and other essentials. There seemed to be such an unholy mixture of things practical and ornamental in real old cottages that I slipped a tin of shoe polish and some cough mixture into Mrs Smith's array.

She has a weak chest and keeps some laudanum by her bed and doubtless thinks she is not long for this world which would account for all the religious mottoes hanging in pokerwork frames. I didn't think she would have a table and chair in her bedroom unless there was good reason, so I decided she took in sewing to make ends meet. A very worn old hanky was used for the white linen and a couple of stitches through the middle of the folds ensures that the scissors, which are actually only black plastic, do look as if they are weighing the pile down. I took particular trouble over finding old fabrics for the soft furnishings in these cottages (see pages 124-9).

Mrs Jones is a much plumper. and jollier lady altogether with a lace collar and some blue glass beads and if you really want to know, she has some lace on her pink crêpe bloomers where Mrs Smith only wears severe white cotton! Mrs Jones has a fourposter bed which is correct in that they were seen in cottages but who knows how it came up those stairs. She not only has a much fancier wash-stand than her neighbour, she even has a dressing table with ebony accoutrements which include a hair tidy. Of course I put a few wisps of doll hair in it as I can remember my grandmother saving her hair combings in a similar jar with a hole in the lid because hair makes the best stuffing for pin cushions.

One of the great joys of this hobby is stepping into someone else's life-style and deciding to hang up a gardening fork because Mrs Smith grows her own vegetables, or to include a crib and a little child's high chair because Mrs Jones has her granddaughter Sarah to stay over when her daughter Mary is particularly busy. You have to know what sort of slippers Mrs Smith would like and that Mrs Jones would keep framed photographs of her late husband's workplace and himself and colleagues on a works' outing. These, like all the other pictures, had to be hung rather higher and tilted further forward than they would be nowadays.

A Victorian Town House

If ever there was a case of an unrecognizable before and after job, this dolls' house is it. We walked backwards into the plan as usual. Having studied photographs of the way in which the talented David Johnson had improved and finished a well-made shell by Del Mason, Jane and I bought a similar one each.

Our first thoughts were to red-brick the outsides to look very like my real 1905 semi-detached house. But then we got carried away by the idea of an artist's studio in the roof, and that led to commissioning a spiral staircase from John Watkins. The plain pitch roof was changed in favour of a home-built mansard and a large hole made in the intervening floor to take the staircase. We soon realized that the artist would be in mortal peril every time he stepped back from his easel, so gallery railings were added to our order.

During this time, we visited the Victorian Society's Linley Sambourne house at 18 Stafford Terrace, London. The newly built house was occupied in 1874 by the young artist Edward Linley Sambourne, who worked on *Punch*, the weekly magazine famous for its cartoons. The furnishings and decoration were preserved in the most remarkable way by two successive generations of the family. His granddaughter, the Countess of Rosse, founded the Victorian Society in 1958 and eventually offered the house to the nation in 1978.

I don't know what we loved best, the tier upon tier of pictures on richly patterned walls, the grand piano almost invisible under serried ranks of framed photographs, or the lamp with the most swooping curves of pink silk and

On the left is the dolls' house that looks as nearly like the Victorian Society's real Linley Sambourne house in London as we could manage. The starting point was the shell on the right which still has its original pitched roof although some glazing bars have already been removed.

It has been raised to suggest a basement and allow a porch to be added with steps and pillars so typical of Kensington houses of the 1880s. There is now a tradesmen's entrance under the newly-made conservatory. (The design was only copied from another miniaturist's because he no longer makes them.)

The conservatory has a floor made of postcard reproductions of tiles by Victorian ceramic artist William de Morgan. By good fortune, his peacock design panels fitted just under the windows. The strawberry pot and lupins are by Rohanna Bryan and the statue is a 'souvenir' from Italy.

fringes. It seemed as though every window was either stained glass or had a sill conservatory, or both. There was even a fountain as well in the case of the landing. The downstairs lavatory had an ingenious marble hand basin that tipped backwards to be emptied and a packet of the correct crisply rustling loo-paper.

All this rich detail and an artist's house – we were quite overcome. We went into a brainstorming session over our raw shells at home – if we thought in terms of gray brick and white stucco rustication, wouldn't it lend itself? We decided to add a suggestion of a basement, some steps up to the front door, and of course a pillared portico for that Kensington look. The conservatory was attached to the side of the house on the level of the landing. This provided space on the ground floor for a tradesmen's entrance and the much admired downstairs lavatory.

In a fever, we pooled our odd sheets of plywood and lengths of moulding and ordered vast quantities of bottle balusters. A few superfluous glazing bars were removed to get nearer to the original. I messed about with the rough carpentry and Jane patiently unfastened the blade of the electric fret-saw again and again to cut a joint total of thirty arches and eight triangles for our conservatory windows. To embellish the conservatory, mouldings were cunningly placed round the sides where the base of the windows was not absolutely truly horizontal. A set of museum postcards of William de Morgan tiles were used for the interior. One was a panel showing a peacock that went very well in the space below the window. The other was a good repeating square, in the same sort of blues. Jane used more of the floor squares as a fine splash-back to a wall fountain.

The rustication up to the first floor was made by sticking on strips of wood with champfered edges; this involved fiddly cutting round the angles of the bay windows and quite a lot of filler was used. The pillars were embellished at their bases with circles of lighting flex of different thicknesses (incidentally, single strands of lighting flex are marvellous for devising curved glazing bars on fanlights). The roof lantern was built for the studio with acetate and pseudo-glazing bars of plastic railing. The outside of the conservatory was panelled and trimmed with mouldings and a cast metal fleur de lys strip was added to the ridge. Sheets of instant roof slates and brickwork from Reuben Barrows were used for the roof and walls. With all the painting groundwork done at last, it was thrilling to see the finished exterior emerge during one final session when the 'bricks' were stuck on.

Inside there is a faithful rendering of the full-size hall; with Victorian geometrical lino on the floor. The skirting board and dado rail have been painted in the popular rather crudely streaked black 'faux marbre'. Just below the dado, in the real house, there is a Greek key pattern that Jane spotted in the rub-down Letraset series for the dolls' house version (see page 119).

In the drawing room an assortment of components were used to imitate the

An assortment of different wood, cast and plastic elements were used to imitate the rich Victorian cornice. The sludgy green paint and patterned ceiling paper are also as near to those in the real house as possible. Photographs of stained glass windows of a similar period were mounted on acetate for the dolls' house window.

richly patterned cornice and a wrapping paper was found for the ceiling (see page 116). Funnily enough the William Morris pattern paper for the walls was for sale in the real Linley Sambourne house gift shop. In reality the stained glass windows are all on the rear elevation, so we cut a hole in the back wall of the dolls' house to accommodate three photographic transparencies of similar stained glass mounted on acetate. I contributed some yellow silk curtains hung from rings on a pole. They were coaxed into naturalistic folds by hovering a steam iron just above the pinned down shapes. Be careful not to burn your fingers.

The parquet floor is instant wood effect sheeting. A Taiwan fireplace with an elaborate overmantel of shelves was rubbed down and painted ebony black. Jane made the plate shelf that runs round the room by slicing slivers of moulding for its supports. All the other paintwork is a sludgy green. Although the doors are correct in shape they have not yet been richly painted in the panels as in the real house. Wood stained or painted doors are both correct for this period, but if you decide on paint, white paint is the least likely colour to be used for a claustrophobic, heavy, Victorian period setting with all that coal dust flying about.

Between us we managed an uncannily good version of the real lampshade. A third of a ping-pong ball was covered with a flared shape of silk, so as not to have too much fabric to gather up at the top. It is very difficult to keep any miniature draperies from turning out too full. A faded piece of old red fringing was glued on with some gilded pierced brass round it. The fringe was trimmed after offering the lampshade up in the room to decide the correct length. Vertical strips of pierced brass and the coronet-shaped jewellery findings were added to the top. It looks very elaborate, but in high Victoriana it is impossible to out-do reality.

In the conservatory, the 'cast-iron' table and chairs come from John Watkins and the as yet uncaged birds are by Margaret Alford from the Dorking Dolls' House Gallery. We have plans for an aviary using a fine aluminium mesh that is sold for repairing dents in car bodies and gnarled branches as supplied for the Japanese style of flower arrangements.

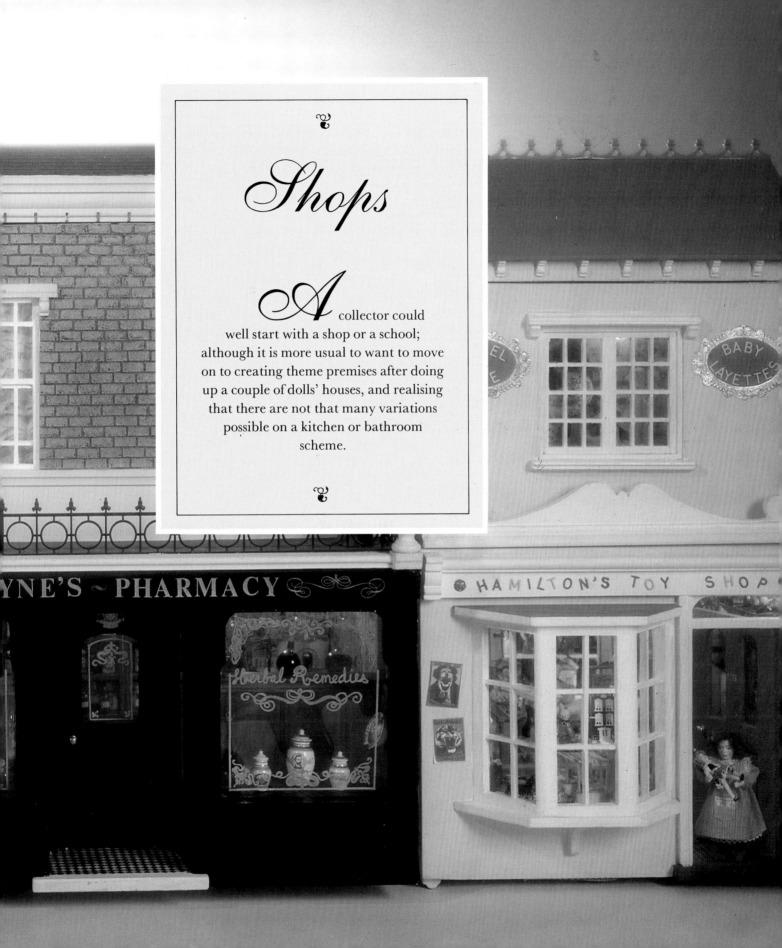

Shops

$\mathcal{A}$ collector could
well start with a shop or a school;
although it is more usual to want to move
on to creating theme premises after doing
up a couple of dolls' houses, and realising
that there are not that many variations
possible on a kitchen or bathroom
scheme.

There are a few miniatures to be proud of in this setting on the *left*, like the gilt and 'marble' table, but most of the objects are my own efforts at painting cast metal teasets and plates, and contriving vases from beads. Upstairs the place has gone to rack and ruin since the roof leaked, the wallpaper went mouldy and the elderly owner has given up trying to keep it in order.

The shops on the *previous page* show three different treatments which can be applied to basic plywood shells. On the left is Mimi and Musetta's Millinery Shop (pages 81–2) to which filling compound has been applied and then scored for brickwork; the centre is Payne's Pharmacy (pages 94–7) which has been decorated using instant brickwork and rub-down lettering, and on the right is the Toy Shop and Layette Shop (pages 74–8) which has simply been painted with emulsion.

Two Antique Shops

Antique shops are a boon to the over-enthusiastic collector who decides with hindsight that various pieces are unsuitable for another house after all. They also allow you to try out techniques for decorating furniture, making up kits, sampling a different style, or contriving wondrous objects with gay abandon as they hide a multitude of sins in their cheerful clutter.

The shops here are another twin project using a pair of double-fronted Georgian shops with curved bay windows by Sid Cooke. The results are Jas. Glasspoole and Chas. Hamilton and once again our different personalities stand revealed in our miniature creations: Jane's is beautifully executed and mine is a jokey muddle with a leaking roof.

The ground floor of my shop is quite straight forward. Chas. Hamilton himself is an elderly gent with a few strands of hair carefully brushed over the top of his head and a diffident manner in dealing with a rather smart lady customer. The furniture varies tremendously from a beautifully designed console table by John Hodgson to a whole lot of cheap and cheerful plastic furniture made in Spain by Mobistyl in lines that were quite pleasingly Chippendale.

It was fun to try my hand at painting white metal castings to look like china plates and coffee services. The look of a lustre glaze came from using the 'metallic' finishes from the range of little tins of paints sold mostly for model cars. A fine three-pronged jeweller's gadget for holding gems is ideal for grasping tiny objects to be painted. More specific to the antique shops was to assemble the handsome suit of armour kit, painted with 'gunmetal' that buffs up when dry to just the right gray sheen.

To paint the console table which was cast in white metal I used a base of antique bronze (which is really a dark brown) and gold ink from a felt-tip pen. The marble top was simulated with vinyl floor tile with a coat of dark green on the underside to make the marbly streaks in the tile show up better. Vinyl is soft enough to bevel the edges by sanding. The edges can be kept straight if the sandpaper is taped down onto a flat surface and the vinyl rasped across it.

The so-called round gold boxes with enamel lids are jewellery findings set in attractively ridged brass screw cups. The oval ones are similar tops with other findings and pieces of pierced brass strip. Some of the vases on the shelves are a combination of a round bead steadied on a jump ring base with a matching cylindrical bead for the neck of the vase. Cloisonné beads in traditional red or black oriental designs are excellent for this purpose. There is a genuine fine china plate with a pierced rim on top of the grandfather clock. It needed to be seen standing properly in a plateholder, so I contrived one out of two dolls' house coat hooks laid on their backs and stuck to a little strip of card at a ten minutes to two o'clock angle.

Having been lucky enough to buy a stack of the cheap plastic furniture in a half-price sale I really could afford to mistreat it. This gave me the idea of

*J*ane's shop has two niches and a French window built into a false wall.

*J*as. Glasspoole's antique shop (*opposite*) is in tasteful sage green with touches of gold leaf to impress summer tourists.

Strips of plastic were softened in boiling water to curve round the bay windows below pierced brass railings. Acanthus leaves were added to the pilasters and the upper storey was given the raised brick treatment described in detail on page 109.

piling tottering pyramids of furniture upstairs and so the theme developed. I stained and ripped the wallpaper I had just put up as the roof leaks and it is all getting too much for poor old Mr Hamilton. I then sprayed the scene with furniture polish to make it tacky and threw some of the contents of my vacuum cleaner bag at it! Not very scientific, but I decided the strands of hair in the dust could be cobwebs and I set off into the cellar to bring up a few real ones to drape over the window frames.

Mr Glasspoole runs a much better establishment. Jane decided to furnish the shop almost entirely from kits as they are very effective if you take the trouble to follow the finishing instructions with care. Her first task, however, was to create architectural interest on the ground floor with two recessed niches and a French window in a false back wall. We worried about over-heating as well as being able to get at the concealed light fittings as an illusion

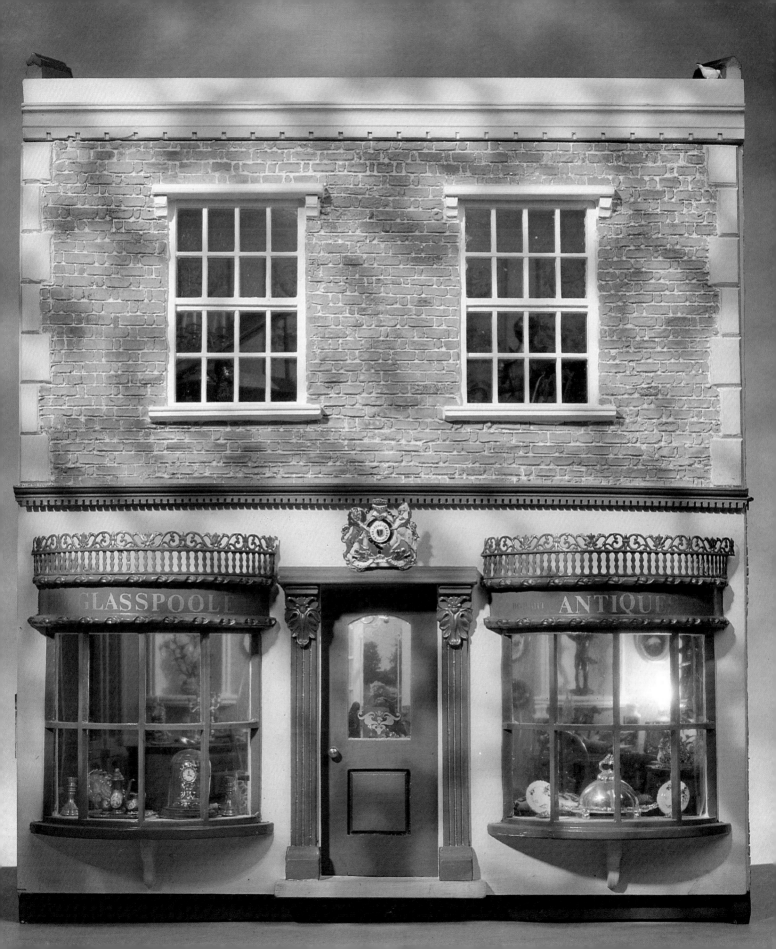

of sunshine was going to need quite a bank of torch size bulbs rather than mini fittings. With some trepidation we cut a large panel out of the back wall which was then papered with a landscape in a suitable perspective which we found after leafing through umpteen magazines. The remainder of the unseen wall was riddled with ventilation holes.

For this sort of electric wiring it is a great advantage to have an English style front opening dolls' house rather than the open back American models, so that the spaghetti junction of wires poking out of the back wall can be concealed without having to plan so carefully ahead.

The pillars on the ground floor are two sets of half round pilasters back to back. They come from a useful range of architectural features from Unique Miniatures in the USA. Jane made the panelled walls upstairs by first deciding to use the motifs on a pretty Florentine looking gift wrap paper, and then cutting and gilding scale mouldings to fit around them. Dolls' house decorating allows for real life procedures to be done in reverse order.

An example of a new use for an article made with another purpose in mind is the etched brass ivy. It is not used as a plant, instead it is used round the outside of a plain china vase as an appliqué decoration. Elsewhere I've seen it used in its raw brass state on plain gas chandeliers which seemed to need more high Victorian ornamentation.

On the principle that antique shops can take anything, there are various humble pieces of souvenir knick-knacks like elephants and Egyptian cats and little pagodas sold to decorate a full-size terrarium or bonsai tree. Odd chess pieces make good statues, prancing horses and military figures liberated from model soldier kits can be utterly transformed by mounting them in plaster on buttons and painting them Tang dynasty blue or antique bronze. I think it is a mistake for a beginner to make something that appears to be in the wrong materials, like a polished wooden coffee pot, but I am not at all purist about there being a wooden turning or a metal casting under some really fine paintwork. I love trying to spot ingenious conversions. Where would the interest lie in looking at collections, if the scenes were solely a reflection of their owner's buying power?

A Toy Shop and Layette Shop

When I had filled my Victorian dolls' house's nursery to overflowing with tiny toys and a dolls' house inside a dolls' house, I thought it time to call a halt and move to a specialist toy shop as an excuse to go on collecting.

The toy shop is in a small house in the village. It measures only 11 ins (280 mm) wide by 9 ins (230 mm) deep inside, so it really only needed to be fitted with display shelves. I had spent about a year accumulating toys for it – I like having a project simmering away on a back burner, as one is far more likely to come across interesting pieces if one is browsing rather than frantically shopping to order. It was also useful to know the height most

Shelves built for this toy shop were spaced to accommodate the toys that had been collected over a year or two. I realise with hindsight that the owner must have a phenomenal memory as there are no price tickets to be seen on the stock.

suitable for the various shelves; bought fitments can be exasperating if they don't allow your toy soldiers to stand up.

I cut a removable set of three arches and edged them in red and white cord to allow me to install some pea bulbs for concealed lighting. A piece of moulding was fixed along the open front ceiling edge of the shop for the same purpose, making the whole establishment a lot more cheery than the one visible 'oil lamp' would otherwise have allowed.

The open backed counter is home-made with scale mouldings, a cornice moulding is upside down as the base, and I used acetate for glass. Wall and floor cupboards on the right are inexpensive plastic furniture painted bright green. My collection of gift wrap produced a delightful fairground and toys paper which is not that accurate in period but far too pretty not to use. The blue 'linoleum' is also gift wrap paper.

The toys are a wildly eclectic mixture. There are six pink hippos bought for next to nothing, a butterfly hairclip with a string and tissue kite-tail added, some model railway farmyard animals stuck on to card as if sold as a set. The rather nasty looking naked pink dolls inside the counter look fine when you have enough of them to look like the shop's stock. The abacus came off a keyring and a furry black and white panda pencil sharpener was reincarnated as a miniature World Wildlife Fund collecting box.

Among the items actually sold for dolls' houses are the plastic balloons, the minute toy soldiers and the pewter cast figures with movable limbs like the clown and monkey and the pull along ram with improbable blue bows. Punch and Judy are made up and painted from a white metal kit and the rocking horse is made from an old white kid glove by Joan Gibson, a craftswoman famous for her eye for the ingenious recycling of everyday materials. My pride and joy is an exquisitely made teddy bear with proper jointed limbs by Anita Oliver – just imagine trying to stitch, reverse and stuff such minute little tubes of furry fabric without ripping the seams apart.

The kindly looking owner has a till and sheets of tissue paper to hand. I can account for his not having a stock book by saying he is hopeless at book-keeping, but far worse than that omission, it seriously worries me that he has no facilities to make himself a cup of tea. One should show more consideration to one's doll friends and think a project through more thoroughly than I did in this case.

The room above the toy shop was fitted out as a baby layette shop to show off some of the adorable miniature knitting that nimble fingered craftswomen produce. I named the shop Isobel and June after two of them. If you have difficulty in finding sufficiently fine knitting needles to try mini-knitting yourself, make some out of short lengths of steel piano wire filed to a smooth point and mounted in wooden dowels for ease of handling.

The working roundabout is a superior Lawrence St Leger toy from The Mulberry Bush, whereas the small pram and the Punch and Judy are home painted from white metal kits. The chirpy looking doll in her box is by Janice McGann.

The lighting from the three visible lamps in the layette shop is supplemented by more lights hidden behind the front architectural feature. In the toy shop downstairs it was necessary to create this kind of baffle artificially. The wallpaper frieze is one particular stripe taken from a gift wrap paper.

The wallpaper is also a gift wrap and there was such a pretty patchwork design paper available that I'm pretending it is a linoleum floor covering.

The armoire at the back is a painted over piece of mass-produced furniture done with great artistry by Moorland Miniatures. I took out a shelf and lined it with red hearts paper and made a little brass rail and some coat hangers to take baby dresses knitted in fine mercerized cotton. The hooded shawl on the rocking chair is made out of single-ply baby wool, but even that seemed a little stiff to drape, so it is pulled down and secured with a couple of stitches round the chair back. The cushion cover is woven out of pastel shades of silk ribbon and the oval mat is crochet work.

The shop fittings are mostly inexpensive pieces improved with shelf lining paper with pinked edges. Some of the stock is just folds of fine pink and blue jersey fabric and there is an interlining material known in the rag-trade as Dump that looks just like soft knitted shawls for dolls' house babies or grannies. I also used some old broderie, and white gauze to represent those

The ultra fine baby garments are made by knitters Joan and Joyce Griffith, Isobel Hockey and June Stowe.

All the papers and tiles are naturally blue in the interior of The Bluebell Bakery (*opposite*). There was so much going on with six dolls in such a small space that the errand boy has had to go away and park his bicycle elsewhere. You are supposed to imagine that there are stairs somewhere behind the 'bead' curtain that lead to the door upstairs left ajar with its opening lined with black card.

lovely soft nappies made before the days of disposable diapers. I fiddled about with tiny bits of tissue stuffing to make the minutely knitted bootees stand up to be seen and made little wooden stands for the matinée jackets and matching bonnets.

Goodness knows how the pram got up there as I was more interested in hanging some beautiful patchwork baby quilts on the walls than in making a pretend door. The pram, made by the Robersons, has full-size embroidery canvas on its sides which makes very good miniature cane-work. The baby has to belong to the lady owner as it has such a lively face it can't be a shop dummy. The finishing touches were minute little china Beatrix Potter figures by Veronique Cornish and some plates commemorating royal births by Muriel Hopwood.

A Bakery

If, like me, you try hard to stay slim and have to banish all those naughty but nice cream cakes from your life, why not replace them with impunity in a miniature bakery? It was an extremely attractive theme to work on, though the small house I had chosen for its attractive bay window made it difficult to incorporate a shop and a working bakery.

Once again, it was necessary to create the illusion of more space than the dolls' house contained in reality. In this little shop I inserted a false back wall to give an opening oven; there is a lower fire door with a grill in it behind which a light can be seen if you look very closely. To the side of the oven there are some crude shelves stacked with sawn up twig logs glued into position. The façade of the oven is filling compound scored as brickwork dusted with lock-ease graphite powder to get the slightly glistening look of soot.

The bead curtains in the arched opening are made from long silky fringing. It was amazingly awkward to tape down the fringe evenly to make a pattern on it with blue felt tip pen. If I pressed hard, the strands slid away from the pen so I had to adopt a jabbing motion which got more ink on the ruler than on the fringe.

As you cannot see how much depth there is behind the false wall, I pretended that there was a whole passage leading to some stairs, so I could still fit a recessed display niche into the remaining small space. With a concealed light and a mirrored back it was ideal for my home-made wedding cake.

Next to some of the beautifully real looking food made by proper crafts-women, my cake does not bear close inspection. It consists of slices of different diameters of wooden dowel, held up by toothpick pillars, painted white and wrapped in silver cake frill. White Christmas glitter sprinkled onto a fine trail of glue and interspersed with silver and glass beads works well for the decoration. The little bride and groom on top are drawn with a draughtsman's pen and cut out with curved nail scissors and there is a little card to say 'Wedding cakes to order'.

Another card reads 'New French fancies' beside a separate cake stand – I had been given a 'tartelette aux myrtilles' and a 'religieuse' kind of pastry which just wouldn't be right sitting in the window next to the doughnuts by Thames Valley and the good old English hot cross buns. There is also a mouth-watering strawberry meringue and a shortbread you could swear was real with minute prick marks and a dusting of 'sugar' by Christine Lincoln.

The bread on the home-made wire cooling rack is baked until brown from a recipe using half plain flour and half salt mixed with water. It is extremely easy to make, but if you want some cut open on a table setting bake it pre-sliced as it comes out rock hard. I favoured round 'cottage' loaves as they turned out better than 'tin' shapes. I did a few apple turnovers and Cornish pasties and found that finely crushed black peppercorns did well for raisins in the currant buns.

The floor of the dolls' house was coarsely sanded to key in a coating of filling compound mixed with one third wood glue and two thirds of water. This was laid on deliberately unevenly and scratched as for slate flagstones while still damp. Once dry and lightly sanded down it was painted light gray first, as the joins look dustier than the slate in real life, then brushed with rather dry darker gray with any excess paint wiped off but keeping to the outline of individual stones. A thin application of a wax polish finally achieved the appropriate soft sheen of real slate.

Upstairs in the bakery kitchen I used a blue squared roll of waxed shelf paper to tile the walls and the long rear counter. The row of pudding bowls are filled with lumps of foam under white gauze to represent dough rising. There is an interesting clutter on the table with a sprinkling of spilt flour about the place and a very unusual lemon-squeezer gadget from Miniature World in Bristol.

To pose the dolls I looked at my posture in a mirror while pretending to heave a pallet of bread forward (using a broomstick), and again to see how one steadies oneself when leaning forward across a counter; the back elbow comes out at an odd angle. The little girl is stretching to hand over a penny for her jam tart. Upstairs the cook has taken more jam tarts out of the oven and, as the tin is hot, she is using an oven cloth. The doll kneeling on the floor was already posed like that by the maker, Joy Dean. I couldn't justify her scrubbing the floor in the middle of the day's work at the bakery, so she was assigned a little broken egg to clean up.

If you decide to have dolls in your houses, they ought to be posed as realistically as possible, even if it means torturing them with pins to make them sit, or making their little china hands sticky with grip-wax to hold something. In my view it is a cardinal sin to have a person on a metal doll-stand in a miniature home. If they refuse to stand up unaided, give them a chairback to hold on to, a mantelpiece to lean against or make a cone of stiff card to place under a lady's long skirt.

The haberdashery department of Mimi & Musetta's millinery shop also sells a variety of fancy 'notions', such as the lace collars and ladies' neckbands displayed on the wall. The chairs have been painted black and re-upholstered in buttoned silk. The inside of the ground floor hat shop can be seen on pages 68 and 69.

A Millinery

Everything about Mimi and Musetta's millinery and ladies' fashions is rather over the top pink and pretty. Jane threw caution to the wind and stuck several curly pieces of plastic to its façade. Inside she first scribed plank outlines into the plywood floors, and got the messy job of staining and varnishing out of the way. The cupboards along the back wall were planned to accommodate a collection of Edwardian large hats. The square brackets to hold the hats were made of square brass cup hooks and covered wooden beads.

The charming little panels that decorate the drawer and cabinet fronts came from hotel guest soap packets. The more prominent hat stands have tripod feet and graceful brackets made from brass pieces bought in a model shop. More pierced brass is used to support and trim the console table on the

It is extraordinary to see how a doll artist can convey a whole character with a pinch of the clay or a stroke of the brush. The little boy standing near the teacher's desk is quite obviously the class toady.

left and to decorate a brass cheval mirror upstairs. The elaborate palm stand started life as two brass corners with feet, originally sold to mount full-size clocks or boxes, but which look great as a jardinière with an extra medallion joining them in the middle.

The chairs in the shop are Taiwan imports doctored with lacquer paint and re-upholstered in buttoned silk and fine trim from mini haberdashers. Sunday Dolls dressed the smart lady customer and her bored husband reading his newspaper (see pages 68 and 69). The clock over the mirror was already quite elaborate with flowers and cherubs but Jane gilded the lily by extending it with extra plastic curlicues.

Upstairs, the haberdashery shelves are decorated with mini balustrading and hold a mass of patiently swizzled up skeins of wool. The shop assistant is winding a ball of wool from a delicate rotating yarn winder by Alan Waters. Jane made the traditional haberdashery counter with its nine little drawers, drop fronted to view the contents. They are filled with cards of tiny beads as buttons, a selection of coloured feathers bought from fishing tackle shops, handkerchiefs with motifs drawn in fabric colouring pens, and flat folds of embroidered ribbon for borders and braids, lace garters and such like.

I made reels for coloured ribbons by using two shirt buttons glued between circles cut out of card, rather than slicing up wooden dowelling in even thicknesses. Another short cut is to stick two stationery hole reinforcing rings back to back for instant circles. Always look for a properly fashioned accessory like a well-made drawer pull before using a pinhead as a substitute. However, much satisfaction can be derived from adapting and contriving if what's needed cannot be bought.

A Village School

Among all the differences in national and regional styles of architecture the building a stranger could most easily pick out, after the church, in any community is likely to be the village school. The belltower on the roof is its most evocative feature. Schools built at the turn of the century in Britain usually had tall windows to give plenty of light in the classroom, but those windows were set tantalizingly high in the wall to stop pupils idling away their time by gazing out of them. They quite often had an entrance for boys and one for girls, and were likely to be named after their founder, a local dignitary or charitable foundation.

My school is called after an imaginary Alderman Higgins because I wanted a nice bluff, no-nonsense name. The building was a small dolls' house designed as a village store, so the windows aren't really high enough and I've had to add half curtains instead. The belltower was made from a notched wooden block astride the pitched roof, some plywood arches and half a ping-pong ball. I glued strips of fine electric flex onto the ball to represent the ribbed construction of the dome and painted it the bluey green of oxidized copper.

The lead flashing round the base of the tower is soft metal saved from wine bottle tops. As an alternative, use heavy foil from a fast food tray dulled down with paint.

My own childhood memories of a very old-fashioned convent school in France kept creeping in and providing me with details like inkwells, slates and chalk. The chalk is made of left-over snippets of white electric flex casing and the slates by painting inside a line scored on a rectangle of wood to stop the blackboard paint. The blackboard itself has a shelf to hold the felt pad eraser and the children are learning the present tense of the verb 'to be' in French. I wrote in all their little exercise books with a fine draughtsman's pen using a tip No. 0.13 which is rather like writing with a needle but ideal for miniaturists. Each is done individually as some of the pupils are better or faster than others – it would otherwise have been handy to reduce and photocopy. In spite of having very French looking exercise books with blue covers and red margins, you would know this is an English school as the poor dunce standing in the corner is wearing a conical dunce's cap, not a two eared 'Bonnet of a Donkey' which is the French equivalent.

Because I was adapting an existing building, there was a severe space problem when it came to rows of desks, so I settled for the fact that it's a very small village and made just two of those typical desk and bench in one sets. The inkwells are white belt eyelets let into the wood and surrounded by blue ink stains. My children contributed the ideas for the graffiti we scratched into the desk tops; some things never change. Some scrunched up paper has been dropped on the floor, but no sweet wrappers as at this time they bought their barley sugar or liquorice allsorts loose in a brown paper bag, if one dates this school by the teacher's long skirt.

The teacher has a hand-bell to ring at the end of break-time and someone has brought her an apple. It is probably that odious little creep standing out in front with the smug look of a teacher's pet. The class goldfish and some germinating broad beans are on the window sill and there are various pictures and maps on the walls. I was very pleased to find a sepia tinted photograph of Alderman Higgins himself, but disappointed not to have found a miniature map of the world with the British Empire coloured pink. I shall have to devise one, just as I will have to work out how to make proper green enamel lampshades heavy enough to coerce those mini light flexes into hanging straight.

A Fishmonger

There are not many traditional fishmongers left in today's high streets, but you may be able to remember one that looked just like this with its large sloping slab of marble that is sluiced down daily, and its artistic array of gleaming wet fish.

In the way that is so typical of this hobby, Jane started backwards,

Using strips of thin veneer to make the panelling, which also runs round the base of the counter, has given the dado in the fishmonger's shop a more pronounced look of planks than would have resulted from scratching 'grooves' onto a sheet of wood. My favourite accessory here is the tub of eels set in resin by Nita Hardy in the foreground.

acquiring the fish before the slab. She was smitten with a collection of fish in a shop and once her eye was tuned in she began to find fishy objects all over the place, both for the shop itself and for the cosy parlour upstairs.

The fishmonger is called John Dory, the name of a fish, in case you hadn't noticed the pun. He is a keen angler, of course, and his living quarters are full of cups that he has won and stuffed trophy specimens in glass cases. His tea of pickled herrings and fish paste sandwiches awaits him and his carpet slippers are warming by the fire as he will have had another very long day in the shop.

I hope you can smell the fish in this photograph.

The fascia board of the shop was decorated with plastic curlicues and a mermaid, no doubt intended as the figure-head on a model ship. Inside, the assortment of fish had become such a dominant theme that Jane abandoned the idea of a cubicle for the cash desk and put Mrs Dory to work at the essential china sink in the corner. Both Mr and Mrs Dory are wearing blue and white striped aprons over their white coats and traditional fishmongers' boaters made of coils of plaited rafia.

The 'tiled' fish pictures on the walls were reproductions on the cover of an angling report. Covered in self-adhesive plastic and then ruled with a grid of pencil lines, pressed down hard, they now look like miniature tiles. The walls of the shop up to the neat dado moulding and the sides of the counter were covered with planking made out of iron-on strips of wood veneer, sold in DIY shops for edging composition boards. The marble counter top is made from a vinyl floor tile. The floor is a slate-effect paper.

Mr Dory likes arranging his counter around his little mascot mermaid on a rock with wet fish on one side and fillets and slices on the other. There is a funny-looking tubful of jellied eels set in casting resin and some shells arranged like foreign delicacies.

A tip from Wentways Miniatures is to coat your painted trout with a thin layer of rainbow pearly nail varnish to get the gleam of the scales. For the translucent white of the fillets of cod Christine Lincoln advises experimenting with a mixture of white and transparent from the range of Fimo modelling pastes. As always, the secret of success is to check the exact shade of any real food you are modelling and keep on kneading and mixing till the basic colours supplied have lost that improbable crudeness.

One of our most brilliant discoveries was how well shattered car windscreen particles do for ice cubes. Picture for a moment two middle-aged women squatting in the middle of a car-park scooping these rounded bits of glass into their handbags with little cries of joy! Of course, do be careful where you stop to pick yours up and only use the glass from a safety windscreen that crazes into nicely rounded particles, not dangerous slivers of sharp glass.

The finishing touches were pinches of model shop lichen for parsley, a scattering of price tickets, a blackboard for today's specials, and a shelf for some jars of pickled onions and a flagon of vinegar.

An English Pub

This attractive corner shop dolls' house is adapted from a building re-created in the York Castle museum. It said traditional English pub to me and a high class food emporium to Jane, so we have one each. Most of my inspiration for the Duke of York pub came from the gloriously rich pictures in *Victorian Public Houses* by Marc Girouard. Indeed, I originally despaired of ever approaching the wealth of ornamentation that was lavished on these interiors. They were designed to transport the man in the street to a far richer fantasy world of comfort and elegance than his humble daily existence could afford.

Before the installation of street lighting, the big copper lanterns outside the public houses were the only source of light in the streets, so my first job was to make one of these. I found a good lantern shape on an otherwise out of scale model lampost, so I cut it off, re-wired it and painted it copper. The wrought iron bracket was made with a curl of coat-hanger wire decorated with jewellery findings, pierced brass pieces and thinner wire curlicues all painted black (see overleaf).

The cosy pub (*left*) is a concept dear to every Englishman's heart and this interior entailed agreeable first-hand research as well as being derived from an excellent reference book. The plump lady in the foreground reminds me of the figures depicted by the artist Beryl Cook who particularly enjoys painting women's shoes and also admits to observing the quirks of humanity in public houses.

The buildings on the *previous page* include the Duke of York public house and Thos. Appleton the grocer's which started life as identical plywood corner shops. Thos. Appleton and John Dory the fishmonger's shops have had filling compound applied to their exteriors which was hand-painted in different brickwork shades. Please admire the mermaid in the centre of John Dory's pedimented façade.

The other exterior decorations are extra architectural features, plastic ironwork for the roof and a lucky find wooden turning for the base of the flagpole. The licencee's name above the door is Wm Bailey, as in the music hall song 'Won't you please come home, Bill Bailey?'.

Inside I built a couple of steps with a newel post and very short piece of handrail up to a small landing and boxed in the corner to suggest that more stairs lead up that way. There is a corresponding false door on the back wall of the room upstairs. The curtained stair archway also gave me somewhere to hide the speaker for the micro-chip music. There are eight tunes including 'Rule Britannia' and 'God Save The Queen' which are supposed to be coming out of a melodion, the forerunner of a modern juke-box.

The interior was a real test of ingenuity as I had not yet tried wood-turning on a lathe and elaborate carving was also way beyond me. I had slowly accumulated all sorts of bottles, glasses, silver-plate and pewter tankards, a possible beer barrel, and a bust of Queen Victoria, so I laid out my treasures and designed a set of shelves to accommodate them behind the bar against a background of milimex mirror foil. The shelf uprights are made of stacked up little balustrading turnings sold for model ships and some fine etched brass railway station strips have been adapted for the front of the shelves. The wonderful curly bits at the top are plastic decorations of unknown full-size origin which have great dolls' house potential. I cut a hole in one with a hot kitchen knife to inset a button clock.

The marble top of the bar was cut from a vinyl floor tile and the curvaceous front has as many different profiles of wood and swags of plastic mouldings as I could squeeze on. The brass foot rail is mounted in model ship deck ventilation shafts and the beer pump handles are a real triumph of lateral thinking: they are small ships' cannon barrels standing on end on top of ships' capstans. Nowadays there are some beer pump handles available in the Phoenix white metal castings. The lamp brackets are also from this range but electrified. The shades came from cheap plastic miniature goblets with their stems snapped off. I pierced them with a hot skewer tip and painted them with red translucent glass paint.

An excellent red flock dolls' house wallpaper from the USA started the decoration scheme and, as it was in short supply by the time I got to the billiard room upstairs, I designed panels to make it go further. A gift wrap border supplied the black and gold dado below the panels. The pilasters are cut from full-size fluted plastic, sold in ironmongers or DIY shops to embellish plain furniture; I boiled some more mouldings to soften them enough to curve round the pillar tops. The swagged and tasselled pelmets over the 'velvet' curtains are yet more of these invaluable strips.

This is not the sort of pseudo rural pub that has horse brasses and hunting prints all over it, but I have given it a Yard of Ale glass and a bagatelle board game. There's a glass case for rather stale food of the white bread sandwich

and scotch egg variety, and an assortment of accessories right down to dirty ashtrays. These have real ash and snippets of white flex for cigarette butts.

A doll artist obliged with a very odd sounding order for a red faced landlord, a barmaid with a bosom, a customer no better than she ought to be and some rather flash looking salesmen. She drew the line at finding them all special clothes, so I dressed them myself, but I do not take credit for the idea of the pickled landlord's longjohns showing above the waist of his trousers. Various other people drifted in like the seedy little lady who cadges drinks, the shy little fellow who likes talking to the parrot and the portly woman drinking port and lemon. To complete the scene there is a lugubrious character standing outside with a sandwich board proclaiming 'The End is Nigh'.

A Grocer's Shop

Thos. Appleton's grocery store is a high class emporium, purveyor of fine foods to the gentry, more a touch of Harrods' food halls than a local corner shop. The dolls' house is the twin of the Duke of York pub's building (see pages 87–93), but given a completely different treatment.

For the downstairs Jane found some museum postcard reproductions of painted tile panels of the four seasons which reminded her of the tiled walls in Harrods' renowned food department. The small dolls' house could not run to quite such vast pillared splendour; so she devised some very attractive wooden framing and wall panels to go round them, stained in the mixture of brown and red mahogany so beloved of the Victorians. She built all the shop counters and fitments herself using a wealth of scale mouldings from Borcraft, with acetate for glass and vinyl floor tiling for marble. A further marvellous find were postcards of Victorian encaustic floor tiles in rich golden yellows, so both floors of the shop are decorated with them.

The patient owner of our local model shop came up with brass railing and stanchions that could be hung upside down from the ceiling to take a profusion of continental salamis, saucisson, rosette de Lyon, Mortadella and garlic sausage. There is some succulent looking ham on the bone being carved by Mr Appleton, who will wrap it in greaseproof paper, naturally, and a particularly nice jar of grouse pâté beside the wide selection of cheeses.

Jane's husband set off the alarm in the London Museum by leaning too far over the rope when sent to gather the detailed information she needed. She did manage to build a good copy of their sloping biscuit boxes on the front of a counter, but the means of devising the museum's overhead string and pulley system for whizzing money and change round a shop has so far eluded her.

A photograph in a magazine of a row of old tea caddies made perfect labels and have been stuck on to wood-turned 'tins'. It is the sort of establishment where a customer would be invited to taste a blend of coffee before purchasing the beans, so that is what the country gentleman in tweeds and a deerstalker cap is doing upstairs.

The ornamental 'plasterwork' on the ceiling is a type of embossed paper called Anaglypta. It was very popular for ceilings and dados up the side of staircases in real Edwardian houses. If you look through the patterns still available, you can find useful dolls' house ceilings that are also very good at covering electric wires.

WOODWARDS
the only
GRIPE WATER

A lady married to a chemist gave me strict instructions to perch a pair of half glasses on my pharmacist's nose. 'They all wear them,' she said.

My personal favourite is the glass jar of little black leeches seen on the right, although I think the real bloodsuckers were usually kept tactfully out of sight in ceramic jars.

Both the exteriors of Thos. Appleton the grocer and John Dory the fish shop were done by creating brick texture straight onto the plywood of the dolls' houses, and then painting lightly in different shades (see page 109).

A Pharmacy

Pharmacies seem to be among the last shops to rip out their lovely old fixtures and fittings in the name of progress, and in most European countries you can still spot the traditional shelves or the drawers with ceramic name plaques, or

perhaps only a set of jars with Latin inscriptions. Even quite modern establishments have incorporated the tall glass carboys filled with coloured fluids in their decor. There is a lovely reconstruction of a pharmacy in the Castle Museum in York and another in the Frans Hals Museum in Haarlem in Holland. I also used an invaluable booklet on *The Victorian Chemist and Druggist* for help and inspiration with this project.

The outside of the pharmacy is the traditional black with gold lettering. Rub down instant lettering sheets include some decorative motifs, scrolls and flourishes that are very useful to dolls' house sign-writers. Wherever possible I advise working on a strip of the right coloured card, or a separate strip of wood painted to match, rather than straight on to the fascia board of your shop. On the fine flourishes always triple check that you have rubbed down every last bit of the gold line. However, mistakes can be patched with the excellent gold spirit-based ink that comes in felt tip pens from art suppliers. These gold pens are also ideal for gilding decorative mouldings and drawing around panels. This ink also covers white metal castings very smoothly for items like clocks or fireplace accessories and blobbing out some ink onto a hard surface will give you a useful paint to apply with a fine brush.

The upper storey of the building and the side walls were covered with sheets of instant brickwork made by Reuben Barrows. Together with his slates for the roof and many other exterior and interior effects like parquet flooring, this is the answer to the prayers of many would-be dolls' house decorators who imagine they haven't got the skills to attempt more laborious processes.

I had been given some gorgeous tile patterned wrapping paper, taken from the magnificent dairy at the Nymphenburg Palace near Münich in Germany, which I was longing to use in a miniatures setting. This complements the Deutsche Werkstätte reproduction paper in 1904 in the showgirl tenant's room upstairs (overleaf).

As old fashioned chemists mixed their own medicines and made their own pills, I thought it would be attractive to include a work area. This was done by pulling the shop's main set of shelves forward from the rear wall and running a 'marble' work top along the back which I made from a vinyl floor tile. For years I'd saved a box of medical ampoule glass maker's samples, so I devised some rather odd looking stands and brackets. I used screw cups from the ironmongers for round bases, some rods and curly oddments from a model shop, split brass paper fasteners and the results of the usual rummage in the 'Come-in-Handy' box.

Filling miniature bottles is extremely tricky as water just sits in a bubble in the neck. The answer is to use a hypodermic syringe, but not having such a thing to hand in the small hours of the night I had a hilarious time sucking out the air and spitting in the water. I badly frightened my husband when he woke up next morning to find me in a deep sleep with green and purple stains round my mouth. I had dipped a pin in harmless food dye and attempted to stir the colours into the bottles with it, but I'd obviously got impatient and blown as well.

The more conventional items in the chemist's are some purpose-made little pharmacy jars improved with touches of gold ink from the fine felt tip pen. There are some stoneware bottles from Terry Curran with wondrous labels such as Universal Embrocation, Dales' Remedy for Epilepsy, Syrup of Figs and the like. There are a few really special treasures among the jars and posset pots and inhalers but the funniest find was a glass jar with little black leeches crawling up the sides. The finishing touch was to cut up a cheap sunglasses' case to make a black rubber door mat advertising Woodward's Gripe Water.

Upstairs, the lodger is a hard-working showgirl, even if she does have the

most appalling taste in furry rugs and mirrored ceilings. She may be a little too dumb and too blonde and too good-hearted for her own good but that's as far as it goes. Her maker, Jill Bennet, contributed the idea of the rather snagged black stockings and her marabou trimmed negligée having definitely seen better days. Floozy has a spangly G-string costume, a large feather fan and some little gold shoes in a fake snake-skin case ready to go to the theatre. She has an overflowing waste-bin and spilt powder on her cluttered dressing table, and who knows what horrors are kicked out of sight under the lamé bedspread.

I have to admit that here most of the furniture is mocked up out of bottle-tops covered in black shiny card and glittery silver panels from a gift bag. The wall lights are quarters of ping-pong balls marbleized to look like alabaster and the central chandelier is a plastic candle-holder. I am constantly surprised at how much earlier than I would have guessed 'modern', or what I think of as 1930s' furniture, appeared. For instance, her ruched blinds, once again so fashionable, were to be seen in a photograph of a 1914 interior.

I found a sentimental-looking pierrot doll for a nightdress case and remembered that my grandmother used to blot her lipstick on a red silk hanky in pre-tissue days, as well as keeping her powder-puff wrapped in a chiffon scarf attached to its centre. I'm not quite sure whether the diamond necklace in the black velvet case is part of Floozy's theatrical gear or whether it is 'real' and therefore the wages of a very large sin. The red rose in a cellophane box certainly came from a stage-door Johnny, and two cocktail glasses seem to indicate that she sometimes has company.

The showgirl tenant who lives above the Pharmacy is called Floozy and I am rather taken with her taste in pink drapery held back with pink plastic doves, not to mention her pink and silver lamé bedspread. I hope you notice that even her mirrored ceiling is included in the picture.

Decorating and Furnishing

There is plenty of down-to-earth dolls' house advice in this section. Of course, it isn't possible to become a silversmith in three easy lessons, real skills are learnt the hard way in any scale. But I hope you will be inspired to cast a miniaturist's eye at materials intended for other hobbies such as jewellery making and model boat or railway building.

*E*very craft is represented in the dolls' house world. Here are miniature examples of glassblowers' art. The blue epergne is by Leo Pilley, and the pink horn vases by Frances Whitmore; the other items, notably the glasses with coloured twist stems, are by Glassblowing of Greenwich.

Starting Out

I have already explained that I think the best way of pursuing the dolls' house hobby is by following your own inclinations. By the same token I am deliberately not setting out a list of tools you must rush out to buy because the mere possession of an expensive lathe will not turn you into an accomplished wood turner overnight. You will either manage to make simple furniture and fittings with straight bits of wood and a needle file until you feel a yearning to go on to something better, or you will decide that woodworking is not your forte and you would rather do glassblowing or soft furnishing yourself and save your money to pay for a craftsman's skill in fields that are beyond you.

The same principles of good workmanship apply in miniature as in full size work and they apply to whatever craft you are involved in. The need to check your references and work out a plan, a careful choice of materials, step-by-step procedure and attention to detail for a good finish could be preliminary instructions to a master carpenter or to a needleworker. You probably know all about them in some skill that you already have. You are unlikely to have been attracted to this hobby if you have absolutely no craft skills at all, so start from what you know and apply it in miniature.

You may decide to begin by modelling food. You progress from plain cakes to wanting to show cook making them. Then it might irritate you that certain utensils are not available in miniature, so you start punching tiny holes in a piece of tin to make a particular grater and you wish you knew how to solder. You go to a full size maintenance manual and find out about it. Next thing you know, you are experimenting with some bent wires and curtain rings and you've made yourself an old fashioned washstand to take a jug and bowl.

It's stating the obvious to say that miniatures are small, but you may need reminding of this to avoid feeling intimidated, and to remember that you do not need a vast amount of expensive materials in order to start. Read as much as you can for full size historical reference, good design and craft skills. If you are lucky enough to be able to get to classes or join a club where techniques are demonstrated, so much the better.

If you are getting ideas from dolls' house hobby magazines, be a little bit discriminating about whether the results shown are of the level you are aiming at. No one makes a silk purse out of a sow's ear and although some adaptations can be brilliant, others still show their lollipop stick origins. You might as well have looked at the real thing, measured it up and started with some fine grained hardwood which will take a really good finish.

Be prepared to make adjustments for the difference in scale. You will notice that sometimes you cannot use the full-size material to represent itself in miniature. Real oak wood often has a grain so wide apart that it looks terrible in 1/12th scale. It may be better to stain another finer wood to an oak colour instead. I have seen the most delightful knotty pine furniture where the 1/12th-scale knots have had to be drawn in brown ink.

A similar problem can occur with carpets. It may well be that real carpets are tufted, but if a real carpet is $\frac{1}{2}$ in (13 mm) thick in 1/12th scale that is 0.0415 of an inch (or 1.083 mm). I've never met anyone who can tie thousands of minute knots per inch on a backing of threads and cut the pile that short. Some form of tapestry stitching has to be the answer if the pattern is to be rendered in sufficient complexity to say 'Persian carpet' to you in the dolls' house.

The only golden rule to follow is to keep measuring to stay in scale. My recommendation is to work in metric where division by twelve is straightforward. If you are stuck with reading instructions that use inches for the full-size measurements, you can use 1/12th scale rulers, or the vast tables of conversions published in hobby magazines. I think the simplest thing to do is to reach for a pocket calculator. To establish the 1/12th scale equivalent of an imperial measurement, the magic formula is to multiply the figure by 0.083 (the decimal expression of 1/12th ie $1 \div 12$). For example, to convert $37\frac{1}{2}$ in to 1/12th scale: $37.5 \times 0.083 = 3.1125$ in. With difficult fractions like 7/8 in you first convert to decimal by tapping out 7 divided by $8 = 0.875$ in then convert to 1/12th by the $\times 0.083$ formula: $0.875 \times 0.083 = 0.072$ in.

There you are, with engineers' accuracy, and you can check your miniature thickness with an engineer's thickness gauge. These are all calibrated in thousandth parts of an inch. Most inexpensive small steel rulers and even schoolroom plastic ones have inches in 1/10ths, which is what you then use to mark out your miniature project from your pocket calculator readings.

It follows that if you are operating in another scale, like the 1/24th, known as half inch, you merely start by 1 divided by $24 = 0.04166$ recurring. In other words $\times 0.042$ is your conversion formula for real inches to 1/24th-scale miniatures.

Not too difficult, but you can see why I repeat that it is much, much simpler to start by taking metric measurements of real objects that you wish to scale down.

The Housing Shell

ROOM BOXES There are ready-made room boxes for sale, some of them with attractive false walls or architectural features already built in. However, if you want to use a room box as a practice run before a bigger project, you might want to build one yourself. The simplest structure is something like my Grandmamma's Parlour illustrated overleaf. It has no frame and a sliding glass front. The easiest way to make grooves for the glass to slide in is to build channels up with stick-on strips of wood rather than grooving out a channel with unfamiliar tools.

It is also simple to make an attractive room box behind a new or second hand picture-frame – having glass in front is ideal protection against dust and damage. There are several ways to attach the frame so that you can open and

shut the setting. A fairly ornate or deep old frame will have enough wood on which to fix proper hinges and a flat hook and eye fastener, providing you build up the walls of your box to a sufficient thickness to take screws. On a slim frame, use a good resin wood glue (properly weighted down while it dries), to fix a rim of wooden strips behind the frame which will fit tightly over the open front of the room, just like the lid of a box. You will need to fix little back leg

Grandmamma's parlour was a packing box for two bottles of wine with a sliding wooden lid. This made a good room shape when tipped on its side with the lid replaced by glass. If you are starting out in miniatures with a setting standing on a convenient book shelf, you do not need an elaborate frame at the front.

blocks under the box to stabilize it. Lazy people who just hook and eye the frame to their box will get their comeuppance when they lift the box and the front drops off!

A room box looks best if the floor is almost level with the front inside edge of the frame, not a deep step down behind it, so take this into account if building a box from scratch. Fix the floor as far up the side walls as your frame moulding is deep when viewed from the front. Thus, the side walls act as stabilizing 'legs' and the whole job looks neat from any angle.

Plan to do any staining, inside or out, before using glue, as this blocks stain from being properly absorbed. Varnish 'floorboards', decorate walls and finish as much as possible before attaching the frame.

To fix the glass in the opening frame front of your scene, use strips of wood rather than fine nails or brads. Either manipulate a mini drill or pin-vice and screw the strips down against the glass with a watch maker's tiny screwdriver, or stick them down with glue and pray you never break the glass, because it will be the devil of a job to chisel out the strips. Hedge your bets and use balsa wood strips which would be soft enough to whittle away, if you were unlucky with the glass.

I used to make shadow boxes for sale, and for these shallow settings, produced in batches, I used timberyard mouldings made into frames that were glued onto three front edges of the box. The top was left free and channelled to allow glass to be slid down into place.

A vignette, or shadow box (*right*), can be simply made behind a frame of timberyard household moulding. This one has been elaborated to include a musical movement hidden under the cradle and a single light that is powered by a battery concealed under the floor. The blanket and bow are pink for a girl and the card contains the name and birthdate of the baby recipient. I am rather proud that one of my boxes was bought for a very royal baby.

The façade of this house incorporates well-proportioned Georgian windows by Borcraft Mouldings. The nicely detailed Venetian triple window was built up around a single arched window kit.

This was the first modern dolls' house which successfully solved the problem of building a basement for the kitchen and other domestic offices which appeared to be below ground level as they would be in a real town house of the period.

A HOUSE KIT   Look at the description and illustrations very carefully before you buy one. You can tell roughly how wide and how high ceilinged the rooms will be from the overall measurements. More rooms across each floor might mean more poky rooms, not really a bigger house. Are there window trims and internal doors included or is the kit made to take ready manufactured components of your choice?

Once you have the pieces spread out at home, stop and think. This is the moment to plan any changes in partition walls or to cut extra openings. Do you want to have stairs all the way up or would you rather fill in the cut out floor and have a bathroom on the top landing, for instance? What can you do with the pieces while they are still flat that will make life easier? Scratching floorboard grooves, and staining and varnishing floors is certainly worth considering prior to assembly.

The Edwardian villas on pages 20 and 23 and the side view Victorian house on page 24 were made from kits that were slightly altered and the house fronts' brick outlines planned before the window trims were assembled.

Another useful tip to consider is hingeing internal doors outside the dolls' house, kit or otherwise. If the cut opening is a close fit to take a standard door (purchased or your own make) it is a shrewd move to increase the width of the opening in the wall at this stage, so that you can fiddle with the hinges and their little recesses (housings) and mount them in a spare strip of wood the same thickness as the wall.

It is so much easier to do this flat on a table than to manipulate screws or small pins within the confined width of a doorway. I nearly wept with rage and frustration over this in my first house, and it seems so obvious now. Then you can continue working on your decoration until you're ready to glue in the fully finished door with its extra little door post. You then cover up the evidence with pre-painted architrave moulding – what could be simpler?

If you have bought a set of plans, many of the foregoing remarks apply, but I would add that it might be a very good idea to cut a dummy run of some of the pieces out of grocery cartons so that you have the opportunity to visualize room sizes or the width of the hall more clearly.

BUILDING WITH COMPONENTS   It is rare to find very large dolls' houses ready made, or a house might not have a particular feature you are keen to incorporate. It is also the technical difficulty of cutting correct profiles or making repeated turnings for architectural features that daunts even quite experienced builders. The miniatures hobby includes manufacturers who have paved every step of the way for you with these products, so study their catalogues and enjoy planning your unique house.

With no more elaborate equipment than a metal rule or tape, a try square and a sharp tenon saw, you can cut out your own main house pieces. A plane is useful to shave down to a marked line if the cut wasn't quite true; but coarse

sandpaper round a block of wood will also suffice. For window openings you need no more than a hand-drill or a bit and brace to make starting holes near the corners and a hand-held keyhole saw if you cannot borrow an electric jigsaw. These are described in any wood-working or house-maintenance manual and can be found in any ironmongers or do-it-yourself shop.

The detail of the hallway of the Georgian house seen on page 30 shows how buying stairs in kit form and handsome, six-panelled door kits enabled a meticulous but inexperienced dolls' house builder to achieve a fine result.

SPECIAL COMMISSIONS If you are going to ask a craftsman to build you a very special dolls' house, this has to be taken almost as seriously as a full-size architect and client relationship. Choose someone whose work appeals to you. Some artisans specialize in a given period and do not find that good ideas well up spontaneously when they're asked to work in an alien style. Others enjoy a fresh challenge and you can probably tell from their initial reaction whether you're talking the same language. Look at the 'Dream' dolls' houses on pages 8 to 17 for inspiration. You will have to decide on what compromises are necessary between real-life and the miniature house.

The more precise you can be in your briefing the better. Don't feel the slightest bit embarrassed to go to a meeting carrying piles of reference books, pictures saved from magazines, photographs of your old home, or whatever. You should save the builder as much valuable time as possible by being as knowledgable about components as you can. You may well have had more time to browse round miniatures shows and read overseas hobby magazines than your busy craftsman. A carpentry expert does not usually do wrought iron balcony railings himself, for instance. It could well be cheaper to agree to have bought-in dentil cornice mouldings than for your maker to try to set up cutting jigs, and so on.

Find out in a straightforward manner what the builder's terms are for preliminary drawings, down payment and expected completion time. Have a clear understanding of the degree of finish that will be included and do not be surprised to find that internal details, like complex panelling, can cost a major proportion of the budget because they take such a lot of time. Discuss whether you will choose all your own light fittings, for both lamps and firelights. It is not easy to visualize all this at an early stage; so discuss whether you would like temporary bulb holders fitted or just some runs of copper tape.

All these guidelines about planning also apply to the way to go about things if you are going to embark on a major building project yourself or with a partner. The finished effect you hope to achieve will influence your choice of material and the order of work.

Architectural Features

EXTERIORS If you have an unfinished plywood house to embellish there are lots of exciting possibilities, so please ban all thoughts of children's toy brick paper. I think a flat coat of paint is also rather a waste of an artistic opportunity, I'd rather see paint applied over a thin skim of plaster or a slightly sandy texture mixed into the plain colour paint itself.

The Edwardian villa (page 21) showed an attractive way of using paints for brickwork, and the Charity Cottages (page 59) also describes the brick effect in some detail. The Pharmacy (pages 68–9) and the Victorian Town House (page 62) were both finished with sheets of instant brickwork from Reuben Barrows. This can be cut with scissors and glued on

Previous architectural training helped Kevin Mulvany develop a shrewd eye for adapting available plastic mouldings into uncannily accurate French architectural features (see page 13). The wonderful 'wrought iron' balcony is copied from a Versailles house of the nineteenth century by John Watkins, a retired metal work teacher.

with a white glue (don't use a spirit glue because it starts to dissolve the textured material if you are over generous with the glue at the edges). Another possibility is the American range of brick and stone effects that work by spreading a compound over a punched out tape of brick shapes. You pull the tape up to leave a grid of 'mortar' recesses.

Take a good look at your dolls' house and compare its features to real houses. For instance, the same plain Georgian dolls' house front might have lines that would allow you to think of it as being in golden yellow Bath limestone, in grey blocks of dry Welsh slate, in eighteenth-century timber framing with weatherboarding or completely different again in red brick. Does it need a few extra features like a porch or a piece of moulding running across the front like a string course? Should you plan to add upright dress bricks over the windows, or an apron of contrasting bricks below them? These can be simply made in thick card, just to get some interesting changes of level in the surface before you paint.

The French house (page 13) has charming details made by adapting

*T*he detail of the Edwardian villa's exterior shows the way guidelines for bricks were scored in the wood and then filled in with artists' oil paints in a lively, traditional brick pattern.

plastic mouldings to look like carved stone. Look at the detail of the balcony shown here and you can see how they have been cut to fit in one direction and softened in boiling water to allow them to be curved into shape for the balcony supports. By choosing carefully, the builder got incredibly near to the details on the real house he was using as a model.

The outside of Thos. Appleton, the Grocer's shop (pages 88–9) and John Dory, Fishmonger (pages 68–9), were both textured by Jane – it is no great labour on such small houses. There's a fine example of the following technique in the photograph of the large Victorian house by Derrick Piper on page 10.

Most countries sell some sort of white plaster filling compound for repairing small holes in full-size walls. We used the powder form that you mix with water. If you use two thirds water and one third of a strong white woodworking adhesive, you will get a mixture that will adhere to wood straight away and withstand years of rough handling.

If you want to imitate brickwork, you first have to answer a whole set of questions concerning period, style, colours, and bond. Refer to full-size reference books as always. In the sixteenth century, the mostly red Flemish bricks were longer and thinner than the $2\frac{1}{4} \times 8\frac{1}{2} \times 4$ inches that became the standard in the eighteenth century. After 1850 the brick tax levied in Britain was lifted and a huge variety of coloured and shaped bricks became fashionable, even on quite humble houses.

The next stage is to decide on the bonding – the way the bricks are laid. Are they Flemish bond: long and short, laid flat? Or Chinese bond: long and short, standing up to look taller? Will you want to embellish your window and door openings with some dress bricks, a rubbed arch or some stucco? Have you discovered 'vermiculated rustication' – the name for the sort of fake stone work that does indeed look like worm castings? Try out some stone and brick work on a spare piece of plywood and you will start to see all sorts of possibilities for walls and floors too.

If your window frames are fixed into your house façade, it is cleaner to paint them first and when dry, place masking tape over the edges that meet the brickwork. Make a card spacing guide for each long, short and thickness dimension and lay the house down so that you are working on a flat horizontal surface. Then smear and smooth on the filler with a palette knife or a flexible kitchen spatula. It is best to mix up small quantities at a time, to cover a single storey, one room size façade or whatever division is formed by windows or string courses of brick to make a convenient section to work on.

With your reference picture propped up nearby, pencil on a few guide lines, especially to make the long horizontal lines true. To scratch the brick outlines in the fast-drying plaster, you will find you wear out toothpicks quite quickly; you can use a fine skewer or the eye end of a thick darning needle stuck in a cork. Use a ruler for all the horizontal lines first, don't worry about mistakes – you can fill them in with a light smear of fresh plaster and go over that area

again. Neither should you worry about untidy little curls of surplus plaster at this stage. When a whole façade is marked out and dry, you sand it quite briskly with medium-grade paper wrapped round a block of wood.

Now you can decide to have a plain colour wash finish if that suits your style of house, it will still have been thoroughly worthwhile to give it the brick texture. If you are going for actual brick colour, say for a Georgian house, in reddish bricks, give the whole façade an undercoat of sludgy mortar colour in water-based paint. Brush it especially well into the grooves. Check real brick colours carefully; red brick does not mean crimson paint. You will be using Indian red, burnt sienna and burnt umber and a touch of ochre or green-gray. Mix little dollops of four or five different shades of oil or acrylic paints, use a flat brush the thickness of one brick and away you go; quickly skimming over random groupings of brick with each different dip of the brush.

If you are making a very distinct pattern of 'blue' bricks among the red, pencil this on so as to leave them out provisionally. Use the paint very thinly and do not despair if it looks terrible until a whole section of varied shades is complete. Step back from the finished house and decide whether it needs a bit of green lichen or rising damp or other signs of weathering.

It really is much more difficult to describe than to do. You will feel real artistic satisfaction at the end of it all and never dream of buying a sheet of boring brick paper ever again!

INTERIORS Trying to make an empty plywood box look like a convincing piece of period interior architecture in miniature will need careful planning. Don't begrudge any of the time you spend looking at real-life examples or researching in books: this is where the dolls' house hobby side-tracks you into richly rewarding byways.

Georgian or Victorian exteriors are very popular with the house builders but it is usually too costly for the maker to trim the interior with the correct skirting boards, cornices and architraves. In any case, how does he know against which wall you fancy having what sort of a chimney breast or how richly detailed your room needs to look? Jane has made a very creditable copy of the bedroom fireplace in the real Linley Sambourne house which just looks that much more 'right' than any bought one could have done (opposite).

My early efforts tended to be distinctly plain and square with a bought fireplace stood against a flat wall, but I began to notice that other collectors achieved so much more with optical illusions of greater depth and interest with a false wall here and a half-open door there. Now I spend much more time with the kitchen scissors and old cereal packets offering up different possibilities like fireplaces across a bedroom corner, false wall and alcoves or a kitchen range in a recess.

However strongly I would advocate careful assembly of suitable components and characteristic elements for the dolls' house version of your

*O*ften the feature in the room which most strongly defines the historical period is the fireplace. If you cannot buy the style you need, do not compromise, but resort to mouldings and the mitring block. Here a copy of the bedroom fireplace of the Linley Sambourne house (pages 63–7) even has home made tiles impressionistically painted with the odd genuine windmill recurring.

The circular chapel of Rowan Lodge has a stained-glass window that can be seen in the exterior view of the house on page 8. The curved surface and limited amount of wall space gave rise to the free-standing prie-Dieu made of boxwood. There is a minutely printed Bible from Gutenburg, the famous press which printed Luther's controversial German translation of the Bible.

The light fitting is home-made from a tabletop candelabra turned upside down and electrified with slim candle bodies and flame pointed bi-pin bulbs.

chosen period, do remember that planning in miniature allows you to take liberties like closing up a doorway because otherwise the beautiful hallstand you have already acquired wouldn't fit on the landing and similar second thoughts.

In practical ways too, dolls' house decorating allows you to 'cheat'. You can paint the skirting boards outside the house and glue them in place after you have wall-papered. You can raise your ambitions once you've realized that you can work quite conveniently on complex wood panelling on a flat surface that will later be slipped into place to line the walls.

A real house often has a staircase that continues up the rear of the house after the first floor, so in a shallow 'cupboard' dolls' house you can opt to scrap a floor's worth of stairs and fit in another small room, merely implying a rear landing by a strategic fake door. In one of the Charity Cottages (pages 59–63), Mrs Jones' side had no stairs at all. I built forward a little section with an open door that gave me a glimpse of a lobby and then added a triangular wedge across the ceiling corner to suggest the underside of a flight of stairs. To be consistent, I put a door on the rear wall of the bedroom.

The dull inside walls of the Almshouses were roughened up with a very free hand application of 'plaster', the favourite filler compound and wood glue mix. Something still seemed to be missing inside the charming high gables of the bedrooms, so at this very late stage I added some structural interest with fake beams. Each beam is made out of two strips of veneer (these are often sold as iron-on floor planks for dolls' houses). The straight edges meet at 90 degrees and the outer edges are cut away a little jaggedly to look hand hewn against the plaster.

I am forever raiding hardware stores for those ornate plastic strips and curlicues that are sold for other people to 'Louis XIV' their full-size bedroom furniture. Swags have been painted brown to look like carving on the front of the Duke of York's bar, other bits were boiled and curved for pilaster capitals in cream and gold, favourite acanthus leaf shapes crop up inside as mantelpiece corbels or outside as extra stonework. The pink hatshop even has them as ornate glazing bars. American miniaturists have more ready-made components available, but necessity can be the mother of very satisfying inventions.

Lighting

I hope you decide to have lights in your dolls' house – I think they are magic. If you have a very old house look to see if there were any recesses at the fronts where the doors hinge on, or whether you could make a very discreet baffle out of card under the front edge of the floors to take concealed lights. A few holes tucked away for the flex would not be sacriligious – this is a method often used in museums.

For a house of this century that could have electric lights for its furnishing period, you will not do any irredeemable harm by drilling a very small hole in the centre of the back walls of the rooms, just below the ceiling, to take a fine flex straight back from a simple hanging lamp without interfering with any original papers. The lamps themselves could be deliberately clumsy torch bulbs to keep to what might have been fitted for use with a battery. Sea View (page 38) has this sort of lighting.

I once restored a lighting system in a 1910 house that had 25 lamps (including the ones in the fireplaces) with 25 separate magnificent brass switches the size of birds' eggs. The original flexes ran under the most astonishing lift-up floor boards and up to the roof through hollow chimney breasts. For this house I saved some of the old fashioned silk covered flex for the short 'visible' lengths that hang down. You could cover a length of modern flex in a black tubular shoelace if you can't find 'old' wiring. Little pleated paper cups for fairy cakes were very often used for dolls' house lights, so do not try to be inappropriately sophisticated with your fittings.

Torch bulbs or similar pea bulbs for use in cars come in 12 volts which is the same voltage as the output of most of the transformers used for dolls' houses in the UK and USA. The only snag to watch out for is that these larger bulbs consume about 300 milli-amps, so you could only run three or four off one of the smaller 1-amp transformers. You might have to search for a larger capacity transformer if you wish to light more bulbs.

As long as you can change a plug, you can wire a dolls' house. For wiring with fine two core flex, as described above, on a house where the back stands against a wall, you only need to lead a number of individual wires to a simple connector block fixed to the back, the base or inside a lift-off roof. Another flex then goes from the connector block to a fused transformer and thence to the real-life power point.

If a transformer is not fused, you would be well advised to interrupt the flex immediately after your connector block with a simple fuse fitting that you can buy from an electrical shop. This saves your expensive transformer from accidents that can happen when tiny little exposed wires coming out of small fittings get twisted and cause a short circuit. You can avoid an obvious danger point like an extension to a flex by using a section of connector block if it's outside the house. If the join is behind a skirting board or under a carpet, always cut one wire back, so that the joins of twisted together exposed wire on the two cores of the flex are never next to each other. It is good practice to dab a bit of solder on joins but not essential. Tape the wires down onto the back of the house with masking tape and hide the whole lot with a sheet of card or pretty paper fixed with drawing pins.

There are three different kinds of connections or sockets for bulbs commonly found in dolls' house light fittings. There is a small bulb which has the very fine flex growing straight out of the glass. The bulb is called 'grain of wheat' if it's short and round, or 'grain of rice' if the bulb is pointed. There is a

The wall lights made of quarters of ping pong ball marbleized to look like alabaster that throw light on the messy dressing table in Floozy's room (see page 96) are typical of Art Deco.

It is not always so easy to decide which lighting method to use for a particular period as the shift from oil to gas to electricity happened very gradually, frequently encompassing two systems in the same house, and some areas never had gas lighting at all.

choice between white plastic covered flex that you strip back or even finer copper wire tails where you burn off the insulation. These bulbs burn for 10,000 hours, but if one does burn out you have to rewire the whole fitting.

The second kind of bulb comes in a very small screw socket with a replaceable screw base bulb, which is excellent in white glass globes or under shades, but looks clumsy if it's pretending to be a candle. The third kind of bulb is also replaceable, round or pointed as before, and is called a bi-pin bulb. This means two short and relatively rigid wires stick out of the base of the glass and are inserted into minute metal-lined holes in a plastic receptacle which then has fine trailing wires. The ones I prefer are white candle bodies with flame shaped bulbs made by the Mini Electrifier in California. See them in the chapel in the Gothic Castle (page 112). All these bulbs are rated at approximately 60 milli-amps, so you can run about 16 off a 1-amp transformer.

I once wired a big charity house after the six smart interior decorators had finished furnishing it and just before the press launch was about to start, so take my word for it when I say one can have second thoughts about putting lights into a dolls' house! If you have any scraps of mini wallpaper left over, gently tear little strips to hide flex on side walls and ceilings. The torn edge glues down less visibly than a cut edge. Otherwise stick to poking wall bracket wires straight out of the back or go down a table leg and under a carpet. In the Thatched Cottage (pages 18–19) wires were painted to camouflage colours where I couldn't avoid crossing the exposed floor.

Of course it's better to plan a lighting system before you start decorating the interior and there are very useful instruction booklets on the subject obtainable from the suppliers of mini systems. For houses to be seen in the round or ones that swivel on a turntable to reveal an open back, most people opt for the copper tape system although fine flex can be concealed in grooves in walls and ceilings. Copper tape is made in self-adhesive rolls for laying a flat electrical circuit that can be papered over on walls or ceilings or laid under the floor finish.

This is not without its problems as it tears easily, needs special connections for the lamp tails to link into it and can oxidize into a disconcerting green stripe if you were over-generous with the paste on thin paper (mask off the strips first). However, it is very widely used and if you are wiring a modern light into a modern wall socket in your dolls' house then you can buy little working plugs, sockets and switches in this range.

For actual light fittings there is quite a lot you can do by buying spare bulbs and contriving shades, as in the Linley Sambourne house (page 66), or make Fimo modelling paste candles like the ones in the Thatched Cottage (pages 18–19). Another idea is shown opposite from Floozy's room above the Pharmacy (page 96). I made wall lights from marbleized ping pong ball quarters. Instead of paying for someone else's labour threading beads on a bought chandelier, you could buy an inexpensive fitting and string hundreds of tiny beads onto it. Jaf Miniatures in the USA have thought everything out for you and sell every jewellery finding known to man as well as providing instructions on how to apply them in making candelabra and chandeliers.

I've mentioned firelight several times in the house descriptions. I love seeing a cosy glow and have massacred fixed fires with a drill in order to be able to insert bulbs. Try placing your own coal or logs over orange tissue paper in open firebaskets. There are some wonderful flickering fire units to buy; some come as bulbs, others come complete with their own coals. Do scatter some ash around to add realism to your hearth.

Painting & Decorating

PAINTWORK The same rules apply as for full-size painting – boring preparation pays off. Unfortunately the small scale magnifies faults. Use thinned down water-based emulsion paint as an undercoat to raise the grain of the wood which will show you how much rubbing down with fine sandpaper is

*A*nything that can help transform a plain plywood box into a complex period interior should be eyed for miniaturist possibilities. Plastic strips and curlicues made by Shortwood Carvings can be combined with 1/12th-scale wood mouldings or cast friezes. Museum postcards and gift wrapping paper are sometimes richer looking than special dolls' house papers.

needed. The little sample pots of paint are very handy, but the stubby brush built in to the lid of some brands is too coarse for anything but ceilings. The small tins of Humbrol or similar enamel hobby paints come in matt colours which look better than gloss in most dolls' house situations. They can also be applied directly on to wood. Treat good quality brushes with loving care and ban any brush that sheds hairs or you'll find an enormous looking whisker spoiling your final coat.

Enjoy browsing through books on the sympathetic restoration of old houses or the history of interior decoration to help you find what colours were popular at what period. For example, in British towns in the coal polluted nineteenth century a practical chocolate brown was all pervasive. The availability of chrome for yellows gave rise to the popular Brunswick green of Victorian taste. Notice the detail of 'faux marbre' so frequently found on Victorian skirting boards. Brilliant white looks too harsh in most small settings, even if you aren't going in for an antique look.

The ceiling of the great hall of the Gothic castle (described on page 54) was composed of individual decorative squares which were painted and then picked out in gold with a felt tip pen. The wooden mouldings between have strips of pierced brass as extra decoration, as does the hanging lamp. It is impossible to outdo the complexity of Victorian ornamentation, no miniaturist need worry about going too far.

If you have the option, paint all your skirting boards, door surrounds and cornice strips outside the dolls' house. Jane did not lie on her back to pick out Linley Sambourne's bunches of grapes in purple – she painted them before she stuck them in. At the very least, tip your house upside down to help you see what you are doing.

CEILINGS Embossed paper is a boon for the novice decorator as it gives a very satisfactory look to a pub ceiling or a period setting. Think of lining ceilings with a layer of mounting card or thin ply. This can both hide newly introduced electric wiring and make it very much more convenient to do

Patterns on early linoleum were often an imitation of other floorings, so it is possible to see red Turkish carpet or golden yellow earthenware encaustic tile patterns as used on the landing of the Linley Sambourne house.

There was a turn-of-the-century vogue for marble paint effects on skirting boards and dado rails. All-pervasive coal dust from fires on all floors influenced the choice of dark colours.

clever things. Cheap jewellery chains and findings can be stuck down in gracious arabesques for an Adam ceiling, and there are always the plastic curlicues, especially for centre roses. Specially made miniature products, such as the complex vacuum-formed mouldings used in the Gothic Castle, are available in the USA.

FLOORING While you still have the flat pieces of any dolls' house in front of you, it is worth thinking ahead to what sort of flooring the house will have. If the answer is boards with loose carpets, there is a very economical way of preparing this effect. Clamp the floor piece onto your work surface and use a steel ruler (or the hardest strip of wood you have) and a craft knife to score lines to scale with the width of planks you are seeking to imitate. The length of plank is then suggested by lines across, remembering that floorboards are usually laid with the joins coming alternately together on a joist running underneath. Tap two or three little indentations either side of a 'join' to suggest where the oval nails have been driven home.

Next, paint on a generous coat of woodstain which runs into all the grooves and instantly brings your floor to life. When that is dry, give it two coats of varnish. I have seen a clever parquet inlay done on a sheet of ply by a builder who varied the stain between light and dark to emphasize the geometrical motif. The different stains did not cross the craft-knife grooves. Floorboards and 'stone' or 'slate' made out of filling compound (see page 109) can also be done in a ready-made house, providing you get this messy job out of the way before you decorate.

Other possibilities are strips of iron-on wood veneer, fancy sheets of parquet in wood and simpler imitation sheets as seen in the Linley Sambourne house (page 66). Also used in that house were postcards of tiles on the conservatory floor, and that idea can be seen with different tiles in the Grocer's shop (page 92). There are stone flags for sale as used in the Georgian kitchen (page 33).

PAPERING Use ordinary wallpaper paste. Size the walls with paste first to give you more slip when you paste up thin papers. One of the best uses I've heard of for a credit card is to use one to smooth down your paper. I'd advise cutting the paper at the corners of rooms as one does in real life.

Purpose-made ranges of dolls' house wallpaper are sometimes not sufficiently rich looking or not available in the style that is needed. For this reason, keep a collection of gift wrap papers, book endpapers or real wallpapers with small patterns.

Sometimes a particular panel is suitable where the rest of the gift wrap has to be discarded for a dolls' house. An example of this is on page 72 in the antique shop, where Jane cut wooden panel moulding to fit around paper motifs. If you are designing your own wooden panelling, you may have a particular overmantel mirror or lights to accommodate which will dictate the

Here are four, very different styles of furniture from craftsmen who are experts in their field. *Right*: An Elizabethan chest made by Ivan Turner. The tower design led the Victorians to call them Nonsuch chests after Henry VIII's palace of that name. Like the original, the miniature has 5,000 pieces of inlay; but on a front measuring 3.62 in × 1.75 in (92 mm × 45 mm). The woods are mainly ebony, box, sycamore, walnut and apple, like those available to the German or immigrant craftsmen in England.

Opposite, top left: A Victorian collector's cabinet in walnut with floral inlay in a variety of precious woods made by John Davenport.

Opposite, top right: A double-domed Queen Anne secrétaire in burr walnut panels with crossbanded edging made by John J Hodgson. The moulding of the domes is also cross-grained. The low boy or side table is quarter veneered in walnut and the ribband back chairs are Early Georgian

Opposite, bottom: A Louis XV bureau plat made by Dennis EW Hillman in kingwood, purplewood and satinwood on oak, with three working locks and keys. The Louis XVI cupboard commode has been made in padauk and rosewood inlaid with ivory and precious woods. It has a marble top and a working lock.

spacing of panels. Serious panelling, as in the Gothic Castle (page 55), is best glued onto a wall-sized sheet of thin ply outside the house and then placed in position. If the panelling is to be painted, use card instead of ply – this looks just as effective and is easier to cut.

Furniture

This subject is enormous, varying from stunning pieces of exquisite workmanship to mass-produced Taiwan furniture. This section looks briefly at both ends of the spectrum, but furniture making is such a complex subject for the amateur miniaturist that it is best left to be discovered in reference books on the history of furniture and cabinet making. There are also hundreds of books and articles in specialized magazines on wood-working techniques.

When seen in a photograph, the best makers' miniature furniture is virtually indistinguishable from the real piece twelve times bigger. This, of course, starts from the premise that they are truly in scale. What is so important for fine quality is that these miniature pieces of furniture do not duck any of the complexities of beautiful furniture in real life. Small does not mean simple. Whether it is intricate inlay, cross-banded edges, serpentine fronts or ormulu mounts, these gifted craftsmen have persisted till they found a way of interpreting these details at the twelfth scale.

The word interpretation is used advisedly, because there is a degree of compromise even at their level of skills. The stalk of an inlaid flower might

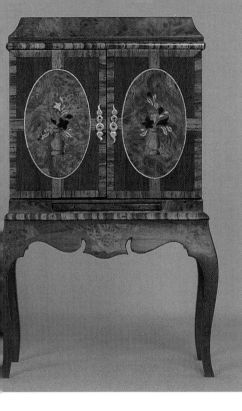

disappear into microscopic invisibility if it were truly scaled down. There is therefore great artistry involved in making subtle adjustments and arriving at a piece which appears totally convincing. Apart from the pleasure mixed with awe that we ordinary mortals derive from seeing these exquisite results of thousands of hours of work, I hope the photographs will inspire new makers to aim for the top.

Furniture built from kits was painted with black enamel and given a final rub down with ultra-fine wire wool. Transfers of chinoiserie designs by Microscale Decals of California were then applied, carefully following the maker's instructions.

Some plans and kits for dolls' house pieces are very good for leading on the beginner, but many of them benefit by being looked at with a critical eye and can be greatly refined and improved as you work on them. Well finished kit furniture appears in Jane's antique shop (page 72). Think of smoothing and softening the angles on the 'knees' and 'feet' of cabriole legs with very fine grade sandpaper and wire wool. Most curves can be rendered a little more graceful with the sort of labour that a kit manufacturer cannot give his product.

Another refinement of kit-building, as illustrated opposite, is to paint a piece in a suitable red or black for lacquer furniture and use some of the fine chinoiserie decoration transfers designed to fit them. It would give you an even richer result if you built up your own gold paint yourself with a little gesso or plaster to get nearer the raised effect of real lacquer. Always sit down with pictures of the real thing as a guide, and you will be surprised at what you can achieve. A design painted onto stained wood with beige toned paint can make a piece of plain furniture look as if it has been inlaid.

Some mass-produced pieces can be sanded down and repolished or have better handles put on them. A couple of hours extra work, spread over a few days between coats of French polish, will allow even a novice to upgrade a piece most rewardingly. If you are not ready to make a turned pedestal table

Examples of 'doctored' furniture: the inexpensive chair on the left was lacquered black and painted with roses in the style of Victorian *papier maché* furniture. For the middle chair, a template of card was padded, covered in silk and 'buttoned' before glueing the upholstery onto the painted chair and trimming it with picot braid. The giveaway red plush of the Taiwan loveseat was replaced by petit point from a second-hand evening bag.

Finely made musical instruments: a lute by Jim Whitehouse, a clarinet exclusive to Miniature World in Bristol, and a music stand from Alan Waters of Australia.

from scratch, buy a ready-made one and then improve it with a new top made from veneer and one of the ready-made inlay shaded motifs that are offered by veneer suppliers. Their patterned strips are also a boon to the home improver.

Be brave about painting a little chair or pedestal table black and decorating it to look like the popular Victorian *papier maché* furniture. Grandmamma's Parlour (page 109) shows this kind of improved piece. The curved love-seat has been improved by re-upholstery. The petit point came from an evening bag (far-eastern jumble sale purchase, not a priceless antique). The design may not be quite as small as it should be for 1/12th, but I thought it a brilliant find.

Simple furniture, like shelves in an alcove or shop counters, are honestly not beyond any pair of hands to cope with. You can use the fine little mouldings sold for miniature cornices to make a handsome base for a counter and the front edges of shelves can be finished with strips of beading. You can imitate a moulded edge by using several thicknesses of thin wood in graded sizes on the pediment of a dresser, for instance, and that saves cutting mitres. However, I do urge you to acquire a neat little razor-tooth saw and a mitring block cutting guide early on if you haven't already been using one for architectural details. DIY double glazing manufacturers make very cheap plastic, almost disposable, mitring blocks which you can use to try things out.

There is a whole industry in painting Taiwan furniture to look like antique painted pieces, often in ethnic styles like Dutch or Bavarian peasant furniture. The layette shop (page 77) has an armoire treated like this. Even if you are no cabinet maker you may have an affinity for this sort of attractive finishing work.

Soft Furnishings

CURTAINS Unless you are furnishing a medieval peasant's hovel, you will have to make some sort of curtains or bed clothes in your dolls' house. Avoid man-made fibres that have a will of their own and use natural linen, cotton or silk that will allow you to coax them into convincing draperies. Mini haberdashery sold for dressing dolls will enable you to find some scale trimmings or you can cut down a cotton lace to make it even smaller. You can swizzle up your own coloured silk cords or fray out lengths of ribbon for fine fringes by cutting off one selvedge. If your curtains are to hang drawn back at either side of the window, be as skimpy as possible with the fabric.

In the first half of the nineteenth century it was fashionable to use very thin, diaphanous white fabric, often combined with a plain silk pelmet, and the curtain drops were often tied back once if not twice. This is a boon to the dolls' house curtain maker who can use fine Indian cotton and soft lining silk, and keep the folds under control with tie backs. Even the later patterned fabrics were not lined, so at least you are only contending with one thickness in the miniature version. Liberty lawn have several very useful patterns, including the famous William Morris period birds in dark colourways that look just like a 'heavy' fabric in 1/12th scale. There is a very good stretchy jersey, much finer than jogging suit velour, that does very well for velvet in miniature. Cast a fresh eye at old-fashioned lacy-knit underwear, to me it said crochet bedspread without the hard work.

If you are not keen on fine sewing, glue or iron turnings with cut down strips of heat-activated vilene. If you are going to use glue, avoid the white rubber glues that turn disastrously brown after a time. White PVA or clear glue are fine if you spread them very thinly on both surfaces, wait till the glue is tacky, then fold up the turning. This will prevent a squidgy mess of glue from penetrating the thin fabric. Patience pays off as usual.

There is a helpful gadget like a hypodermic syringe or very fine cake icing dispenser which helps control the flow of glue. After leaving a fine line of glue to get tacky, roll up a very small hem round the tip of a needle. If you don't want a turning at all because you wish to add a very fine lace or other trim almost to the very edge of your fabric, or the minute hanky or tea-towel is just too small, then prepare the piece with a fine line of Fraycheck which does what its name implies. Touch it to the actual cut edge and leave it to dry. Try it out on a scrap first, just in case your fabric shows a mark even after a very sparing application.

To make a simple gathered heading that is going to be visible, hanging from rings on a pole, for instance, I would advise using three or four rows of gathering stitches on a curtain you have prepared by turning in all the edges to its finished length. If you have ever seen a smocking pattern you will know that you are guided to pick up a regular series of dots; say, about two threads of fabric every 3/8 in (10 mm) or less, depending on the fold you want. Instead of passing your needle in and out of the fabric, you skim along the inside picking up a tiny stitch at a time, and repeat this for several rows, keeping regularly below the previous line of dots. Using this method, the fabric will draw up naturally into folds with no out of scale sewing threads showing on the right side. You can repeat a temporary row at the hem to help you lay the curtain out on the ironing board, or use a lot of pins. Then hover a steam iron over the curtain, keeping your fingers well away from scalding hot steam. Leave the curtain to cool and dry in its folds before removing the pins.

If you are making a number of curtains, bed valances, dressing table skirts and dolls' clothes you can make very good use of a gadget called a mini-pleater. This is a corrugated rubber board with a set of grooves into which the fabric is tucked to make regular folds when it is ironed. Mini-pleaters come in three sizes of groove, known as 1/4 in, 1/2 in and 1 in, and various lengths, for short frills or long curtains. You can iron a strip of self-adhesive vilene interlining material across the back or just along the top to hold the pleats. Although I think there is nothing to beat the smallest mini-pleater for tiny flat-pressed knife pleats, I am a little wary of the over-regular heavy look that

Here you can see a very fine hexagonal patchwork and bed linen made of an old handkerchief. The top and back layer of the pillow case were cut from opposite corners of the hanky to give two ready-turned corners of open work edging. The chair cushion is loosely filled with salt to accept a properly sat-upon impression.

finishes up looking more like real modern curtains with pinch pleat heading tape than the skimpy look that was customary in a modest cottage. For these I would rather run a few lines of hand gathers, then wet the curtains thoroughly and coax them to drip dry into a few soft folds.

EDGINGS   For edgings, you can use silk necklace threading cord. As the colour choice is limited, you can dye it, or alternatively make very good multi-coloured cording yourself using embroidery silk or cotton floss. This is also very useful for tie-backs with a knot and tasselled end. If you need a quantity of fine cording for the seams of an upholstered suite of furniture, for instance, it can be very tedious twisting together long lengths of yarn which then jump together to a cord of half the original length. The answer is to use a hand driven or electric kitchen beater! Fix one end of the very long threads to a firmly planted drawing pin, retreat across the room, tie the other end to one loop of the beater and start swizzling. If you really are doing yards worth, it is handy to have an accomplice to hold the midway point taught while you get the beater back to the drawing pin end before unfastening the ends and allowing the swizzled threads to jump together into the twisted cord.

FINISHING TOUCHES Another unorthodox sounding tip is to fill bed pillows and scatter cushions with salt, raw semolina or grains of rice rather than wadding. They flop so much better over the arm of a chair and can be indented for a doll baby's head, or left looking convincingly sat-upon in a chairseat. I did this in the Charity Cottages (pages 58 and 61) where I also spent a long time trying to get the bought patchwork quilt to hang correctly on the fourposter. I removed a too stiff polyester cotton lining and then cut back all the little seams with fine nail scissors. After remaking a fine hem, I soaked the quilt in almost neat fabric softener. It dried with the patches looking a bit puffy and therefore much more 'quilted' than when I had bought it all neatly ironed flat.

When you want to get a table cloth to hang down, you might be worried about putting a wet cloth over a french-polished surface, so wrap the table top in kitchen cling-wrap film first and remember to have very clean hands when you are smoothing and pulling down a snowy white table cloth. If you need to stabilize a full table setting you would do well to make a card cut out of the table top and glue the cloth firmly down to give a stable surface onto which you then gently press grip-wax under all the glasses.

CARPETS Carpets are items of soft furnishing that are easy to get wrong in period settings by being too generous with them. Very few stair carpets were in use until the early nineteenth century, so stairs should be left bare in small Georgian houses. By the time turned wooden balusters were in use in early Victorian times, the stairs generally featured carpets. Rooms began to have larger machine-made carpets, mostly in floral designs. The first 'close carpeting' was richly patterned in bright colours, but this fashion gave way to a lighter neo-classical look with more floorboards showing again.

In late Victorian and Edwardian times, carpets were often large and plain with just a decorative border, and fur hearth rugs became popular. Wall-to-wall plain light carpeting was not generally seen before the Second World War. You can make a good bordered carpet by cutting the centre out of a rectangle of cotton velvet and replacing it with a different colour. On velvet,

Working a carpet like this on 27 holes to the inch canvas means 729 stitches to the square inch. On this Persian design, Sue Bakker also used over-stitching in fine white thread to give sections of the pattern even more definition. Lady Dreerie comes from the Gothic castle seen on page 8.

mark the cutting line true to the grain on the back and cut with a razor blade to pull the pile apart (as one also cuts fur). If you are ambitious, cut more than one 'frame' for border stripes before dropping in the centre. Glue fine tape over the back of the joins and use Fraycheck on the outer edges.

In dolls' houses, tapestry stitching is an accepted substitute for both needlework and pile carpets. It is difficult to render complex patterns on the 22 stitches to the inch canvas that is generally supplied with carpet kits, though the beginner faced with 484 stitches for one square inch might feel that is quite enough. Silk strands on 48 hole silk canvas necessitate 2,304 stitches to the square inch and will enable a persistent needleworker to render subtle shadings and designs. Higher stitch counts than that have major work of art status and anyone not wishing to spend months peering through a strong magnifying glass should stick to using such ultra fine work for very small cushions or a piece of dolls' house scale needlework that they can leave realistically unfinished next to a work basket.

Various jacquard weave or printed velvety fabric carpets are available. Sometimes the fringing lets them down; either because an early carpet should not have fringing at all or because they are too nylon white or too fat and woolly. It is possible to correct these details on the reasonably priced nylon weave variety by folding back and glueing unwanted fringes to the underside. Finer fringing can be made by snipping one selvedge off a grosgrain ribbon and pulling away the threads. Carefully remove the coarse fringing, touch Fraycheck to the carpet if necessary, then glue the new fine fringing to peep out under the ends most convincingly.

Food and Flowers

The modelling paste called Fimo is very popular for dolls' house food as it stays pliable until it is baked at a low temperature and comes in a wide range of colours. These colours need a deal of careful blending to soften virulent green to the right tone for a real apple for instance, and you might still want to paint on a streaky red blush. As always, follow real life as closely as you can or sit with well illustrated cookery books open in front of you. In the USA, there are dozens of round sticks of Fimo for sale that have the pattern of a slice of lemon or tomato or even iced cookies running through them, just like the English sticks of Brighton rock confectionery. These can be finely sliced with a razor and give a wonderfully professional look to home-modelled dishes.

There are fine artists making both food and flowers who swear by good old-fashioned bread dough, so here are instructions and the basic recipe that The Garden Path kindly shared. Use 3 slices of soft white bread to 3 tablespoons full of white craft glue (Sobo in the USA) and $\frac{1}{4}$ teaspoon glycerine. Scrub your hands first. Remove the crusts and tear up the bread. Place the small pieces in a bowl. Drizzle the glue over the bread, add the glycerine. Blend well with a fork till a ball of dough forms. Add bread if too sticky and glue if too dry. Turn out and knead well till smooth, soft and elastic. You may like to have a very little glycerine on your finger tips. From a medium-sized tube of white gouache (watercolour) paint add a 2 in (50 mm) squeeze. Knead in well. Wrap in plastic film and refrigerate when not in use. Only pinch off a very small amount at a time to colour and work with. Keep wrapping the spare dough. If it gets too dry to work knead in a little water.

Whatever your paste material, you will need a few toothpicks and pins as modelling tools. You can make a three winged tip for repeated indentations on a grocery crate full of tomatoes by using dough dried on the end of a toothpick

Food preparation and the consumption of enormous meals almost filled a well to do Victorian household's day. In a real Victorian mansion, the larder, wine cellar, butler's pantry and housekeeper's sitting room would all have been separate.

The food in the window of the Bakery (see page 79) is mainly modelled in Fimo, a coloured paste that stays pliable until baked. The French apple tart is differently made: to a special French recipe of course!

or you can whittle tips on manicure sticks. You will need something that textures orange skins and the like. A nail brush that can lie on its back or coarse sand paper works well. One of the books on bread dough miniatures recommends a wire perch scraper from a pet shop.

Bristles from brooms or fine wire (0.10 size) are good fruit stalks and flower stems. Some covered florists' wire is suitable for coarser plants or spray paint your own fine steel wire. Use varnish or half-glue half-water for glossy fruit and vegetables once the drying or baking is complete. You can fix pink chalk blushes and the like with a matt artists' spray.

There is a whole school of thought that uses green florists' green plastic tape with a spine of wire for house plants; another prefers crêpe paper or fine artists'

coloured card with added painted details. If you would like to make a mass of geraniums, you will find a shaped paper punch or a homemade tool, like a mini pastry cutter, a great help for Fimo shapes.

As there are whole books devoted to every aspect of food and plant making, I will just encourage you to have a go and then progress to the fun of using casting resin for liquids in jugs and glasses, or for bottling fruit in jars. Some finds like coriander for nuts or haricot beans for potatoes will come to you if you look at your own kitchen stores with a bit of lateral thinking. And one final word – in general, try to get the time on clocks to be consistent with the meal on the table.

Accessories

It is very tempting to collect lots of little knick knacks that take your fancy, but you should really be asking whether Mrs Smith, or whoever 'lives' in your dolls' house, whether *she* would like them. Does the lady knit, read or sew? Does the gent play golf or go fishing? What were the sort of pictures they would have had, and – just as importantly – how would they be hung on the wall? Not by blobs of Blu-tak, surely a Victorian house would have had its pictures hanging from a picture rail? A card of carpet thread is handy for this sort of dolls' house string and it's useful for mini brown paper parcels too.

The smarter magazines that carry coloured advertisements for art galleries are a good source of pictures, as are museum postcards. Perhaps you can re-photograph the pages of your family album in black and white. Then the contact strips can be dipped in sepia solution to bleach them to the brown look of old photographs and you can have your own grandmamma framed on your mantelpiece. One clever friend filled a modern dolls' house book shop with all her favourite books. By trial and error she calculated how far away from the spread out dust cover of a book the camera had to stand, so that quite ordinary developing and printing gave her a 1/12th-scale version of it. Your least successful holiday snaps can be beheaded for small portraits in a jewellery finding or a small brass curtain ring.

Keep an eye open for anything small, like the summary of the year page of a pocket diary for a calendar, pictures of products on coupons and in advertisements, pictures of nicely bound books, clock faces that can be mounted behind a curtain ring, Christmas cards in charity catalogues and so on. I mentioned broken windscreen particles for ice cubes in the Fishmonger (page 87) and I scavenged wood turnings for the pub's flagstaff (page 89).

The smallest size of ornate brass box fasteners sold in hobby shops have done duty for roller blind fixtures in Thos. Appleton's grocery (page 92) and others painted black are hinges for the Bluebell Bakery's oven door (page 79). The stud half of these fasteners converted to a very nice inkwell with two brass belt eyelets containing trimmed sparrow feather quills, courtesy of my cat. I mentioned writing mini letters with a 0.13 draughtsman's pen; you can also make little envelopes, addressed and franked, that you then tear open with a pin. If your setting is Georgian you can't have stamps yet, so fold the letters and seal them with a minute blob of 'sealing wax' of Fimo. Do fill up the pigeon holes of a desk with both used and unused stationery, and have some ink stains on the blotter.

For an Edwardian dressing table, I puzzled over how to get jewel stones to stick to the head of a pin for those enormous hat-pins ladies needed to anchor their great big hats. I finally poked a pin through one half of the smallest size of press stud popper fastener and glued the stone onto that head. It is important to have spilt powder and a powder-puff and some 'hairs' in a comb on a dressing table, just as it is to have spilt flour, half peeled fruit, crumpled

The sewing table is the top of a cotton reel that revealed interesting 'compartments' under its label. The pedestal is a salvaged turning and the base is the end of a plainer reel mounted on beads. The contents are mainly home-made. In contrast, the four trays of the *nécessaire* contain ultra-fine sewing and manicure implements made by former jeweller Lawrence St Leger. The boxwood cotton reels on a pearwood stand are turned by David Wadley.

A richly laden dining table set with a mixture of plastic cutlery and sterling silver serving dishes. The background is a carpet inspired by Louis XIV Savonnerie designs in the Rothchild Collection.

tea-towels and oven cloths in a kitchen.

As craftspeople tend to specialize, you may well find you can do something to their original product that will make it unique. An obvious example is to stretch your own 'work in progress' on a bought embroidery stand. Another might be to take two lovely ivory gentlemen's hair brushes, made by a turnings' specialist, and you make them look like an Edwardian travelling set by making your own oval leather case for them. A red rubber hot water bottle is available to buy, but what makes one smile is the knitted cosy cover with a draw string at the neck.

To make a scene interesting and alive you can easily spend as much time on accessorizing as you did on the original building or decorating. You have to be observant and think through every miniature activity and be sensitive to the nuances of the station in life of your inhabitants.

Dolls

There are collectors of fine miniatures who regard dolls as the weak point in perfect scale reproduction and are just not interested in having them. As you have gathered, I love them and believe in knowing all about the people who live in my houses. I get cross when they won't bend at the wrist to perform a particular action and I don't really warm to beautiful ladies who can't sit down or hold their babies properly. One way of dealing with this is to buy dolls in kit form and dress and pose them yourself.

There are many different kits available, many with very distinct characters in their features and it is interesting to see how some doll dressers can transform a mould from a jolly cook to a cheeky boy by different wigs and clothes. If you are not confident about dress-making there are wonderfully carefully thought-out period patterns to follow. You will be greatly helped if you stick to natural fabrics or only use polyester if it is pulled taught in a cummerbund, not where it ought to drape softly. Gentlemen are often harder to dress than ladies as real suiting is hopelessly thick for 1/12th scale. You have to adapt by using dark silks, but then be sure to give them adequately padded limbs under thin fabrics or they will look terrible with almost empty trouser legs when they sit down.

It is up to you to accept the limitations of movement if you need arms made entirely from china for a ball gown or a twenties short sleeved dress, or to choose the shortest hand and wrist that you can find and make long sleeves so that you can manipulate the pose. For this reason, always look closely at the hands. China thumbs and extended fingers are a nightmare for the maker as so many break in production, but the cheaper range often have irritating little paws that never look as if the doll is doing anything.

In the Bakery (pages 78–80), I made a point of talking about movement and adopting the pose you want in front of a mirror and then torturing the doll into assuming it as nearly as possible. Even if you don't feel able to sculpt faces in Fimo or Sculpey modelling pastes, you might consider doing the hands yourself. In the USA there is a growing trend for doll artists to make figures caught in the middle of balancing a pie plate on their finger tips, soaking their feet in a tub of resin water, taking a bath like the miner on page 40 or even suckling a baby.

Be careful to choose faces that fit the period you are depicting. You might think a face is always a face, but it doesn't work like that. We are all

The gentleman is dressed by Sunday Dolls like the Dickensian Mr Pickwick, and the lady's dress is also mid-Victorian. The pram is by Colin Roberson.

collectively influenced by the legacy of contemporary portrait painters' perception of beauty. Think of Rubens' fat pink goddesses compared to El Greco's starving saints or the way all Charles II's mistresses look alike in the Lely portraits. Some dolls have much too much modern eye make-up to look right in Regency clothes.

Never discard any fabric item without eyeing it for miniature possibilities first. Sometimes the connection isn't obvious; a rich tie silk is impossible for a doll gent's tie but wonderful for a chair seat. The best mini-gingham jam-pot covers I ever found came from a boy's shirt. Men's shirting in fine stripes makes great uniform dresses for cooks and nannies. Tartan ribbons are the answer for mini-plaids. Old embroidered ribbon makes good silk waistcoats. Children's bright socks make excellent sweaters and you can cut a snippet of the ribbed edge to use on pins for knitting, trailing a ball made of matching darning wool.

A bow maker is another useful aid. With this gadget, you loop a silk ribbon round two vertical posts, knot it in the middle and slide off a perfect little bow.

Doll artist Marie-France Beglan models each face and paints each freckle. Her little girl is holding an extraordinary mouse nurse knitted on pins by Helen O'Mahoney, the small patient is in the dress pocket. The boy has a lovely bisque porcelain laughing face. He is by Joan Blackwood from the USA and holds a genuinely threaded tennis racket from Miniature World.

If you need to make little roses for hats, you can make another helpful tool by filing off the end of a darning needle to hold the end of a ribbon that you then twist and glue repeatedly to build up the petals and then slide the prongs out of the base of the rose. Fishing fly packets of coloured feathers are another boon to miniature milliners.

Wig-making with mohair or the shiny kind of dolls' hair is very much a matter of trial and error, but here are a few tips. Start with more hair than you need for ease of handling. For simple upswept female styles, spread clear glue on the doll head, especially along the neck and the front hairline right down to the ears. Tie a long hank of hair together in the middle, and when the glue is tacky place the tie at the crown of the head and spread the hair down, past all the glue. Allow it to set, then double the hair back up to the crown, twist and stitch it tightly into a bun.

Ringlets can be set round fine steel piano wire with setting lotion or fabric softener and heat dried before sliding the long sausage off to cut to the required length. Tiny snippets make curls for toddlers or boys and are very pretty to soften the hairline of the style described above. Braids or plaits on ladies' heads are best worked separately, tied very tightly, then cut off near the tie and sealed with glue before incorporating into the style. Little girls with pig tails need a neat parting and a crochet hook is a help when tying the braids with real bows.

Men's hair is very tricky – modern styles are the worst. Beginners might like to stick to balding grandpas and young page-boy styles. You need much more hair than you would believe possible and then you cut and cut to grade down the short back and sides. Partings can be made by back stitching across a hank of hair, then lifting a neat layer back across the stitching to hide it and create a ridge for the parting. Soak the chap's hair with setting lotion and put him in a sort of mugger's stocking mask till it's dry.

Distressing

Distressing is the term used for faking wear and tear to make instant antiques and for getting necessary restoration work to blend in. For a second-hand dolls' house it is pretty well essential to take the high gloss off new furniture which is to sit next to real old pieces, I mentioned stripping varnish off the table in Sea View (page 39) and in the sense of suitable restoration distressing is also necessary, but you need a light touch.

Don't worry about a well-used, worn look and scratched or faded tile paper; there's no sadder sight than a friendly old house ruined with a bright red gloss roof. If that has already happened you can restore it by using a deliberately 'toy-like' tile paper. After soaking sample pieces of garish new brick and tile paper in various bleaches and solvents to no effect, I found that acetone dissolves the printers ink, so I papered first and then wiped over the dry paper with a pad of cotton wool dipped in acetone.

If you have to paint over a replacement piece of wood on a broken window sill, it's worth spending time mixing shades of 'dirty' paint and letting sample stripes dry on a card first so that you get the best match. If faced with a previous owner's disastrous white gloss paint, do your best to strip it off cautiously or at least rub it down and paint over with a more suitable matt paint. Try a bit of judicious ageing with a thin wash of dirty browny gray that you wipe off as you go along to leave the shading in the grooves of the mouldings.

If your new old house has original papers inside that should really be left in place, but you can't abide them, it is simple to put new paper on card instead. These wall linings can be fixed in place with drawing pins covered by little patches of extra wallpaper. In this way, honour is satisfied *and* you have the colour scheme you want.

In a 'new' dolls' house it is a matter of taste and inclination as to how much wear and tear you feel is appropriate. Please refer back to the contrasting treatments of the Antique shop interiors (pages 70 and 73). In the Charity Cottages there is quite a lot of discreet brushing on and wiping off of dilute

ebony stain on the furniture. The new wood of simple items like the clothes horse with Mrs Smith's bloomers in front of the fire was stained with light oak which gives a good, mature pine effect. There are also smoke-blackened bricks – essential for any fireplace. In the pub (page 90), the table was scratched and marked with rings. A pencil that had lost its eraser made a handy ring cutter, dipped in paint stripper.

In the Thatched Cottage (pages 20 and 42) shoe dye was used for unsuitably bright leather and in the study of my big Victorian house (page 28) an inexpensive, scarlet pvc-covered wing chair is unrecognizable under more brown shoe dye. By rubbing the dye off, lighter patches of realistic wear show at the edge of the seat and the arm rests. If you don't need such a complete transformation, you can still add shading round button indentations and where a slightly greasy head would have rested.

Tea is very useful for dulling down a new fabric. Mrs Smith's pinafore (page 61) was soaked in it, then she put it on wet and lay down on a radiator to dry, tightly wrapped in a paper towel to get nice creases. For her simple curtain wardrobe, I was already using old fabric, but wanted to emphasize the folds, so I stroked down them gently with a damp tea bag. Wire wool rubbed lightly over the painted plaster walls aged them attractively. I'm sure you will find interesting methods of your own, though none could sound as intriguing as 'Bug juice' from the USA for weathering exterior woodwork.

❧

*T*ake account of your inhabitant's budget and give a cottage skimpy curtains well dampened to get them to hang softly. This is Mrs Jones' window from the house on page 59 and also shows photographs of the late Mr Jones on a factory works outing.

I hope these ideas will have helped beginners to get going and that they may have added to the repertoire of those already immersed in this stimulating hobby.

As I am lucky enough to meet many enthusiasts from all over the world at the annual London Dolls' House Festival, it is not inappropriate for me to end by saying I hope we meet one day to exchange collectors' tales.

Useful Addresses

From Kitchen to Garret, Magdalen Street, Exeter.

Goodies, 11 East Street, Coggeshall, Essex CO6 1SH.

Jennifers of Walsall, 51 George Street, Walsall WS1 1RS (tel: 0922 23382).

Kristin Baybars, 7 Mansfield Road, London NW3 2JD (tel: 071-267 0934).

L'Atelier, Mansell House, Contree Mansell, St. Peter Port, Guernsey, Channel Islands.

Lovin' Givin', 86 Lower Fold, Marple Bridge, Stockport, Cheshire SK6 5DU (tel: 061-427 7460).

Miniature Curios, 59 High Street, Honiton, Devon EX14 8PW.

The Miniature Scene of York, 37 Fossgate, York YO1 2TF (tel: 0904 38265).

Minimus, 52A Newnham Road, Cambridge CB3 9EY.

The Mulberry Bush, 9 George Street, Brighton, Sussex BN2 1RH (tel: 0273 493781).

The Newson Gallery, 1 Windmill Hill, Enfield, Middx (tel: 081-363 3675).

Patricia's Dolls' Houses, 119 Eastgate, Basildon, Essex SS14 1JJ (tel: 0268 293169).

Ribchester Museum of Childhood, Church Street, Ribchester, Lancs. PR3 3YE.

The Rochester Dolls' House Shop, 68 High Street, Rochester, Kent ME1 1JY (tel: 0634 831615).

Royal Mile Miniatures, 154 Cannongate, Royal Mile, Edinburgh EH8 8DD (tel: 031-557 2293).

Rutland Miniatures, The Old Cobblers Shop, 5 Hopes Yard, Uppingham, Rutland, Leics LE15 9QQ.

The Singing Tree, 69 New Kings Road, London SW6 (tel: 071-736 4527).

Small Sorts, 40 Winchester Street, Salisbury, Wilts SP1 1HG (tel: 0722 337235).

Smalltalk, 96 High Street, Shepperton, Middlesex TW17 9BB

Tollgate Miniatures, High Street, Bosham, West Sussex (tel: 0243 573410).

The Welsh Dolls' House Shop, 11 Brecon Road, Abergavenny, Gwent NP7 5UH (tel: 0873 79113).

Wiggintons, 1-2 St Andrew Street, Hertford, Herts SG14 1JA

UK SUPPLIERS MAIL ORDER

Among the shops which have comprehensive catalogues are The Dolls House Toys, The Mulberry Bush and The Singing Tree.

Carol Black Miniatures, Sun Hill, Great Strickland, Penrith, Cumbria CA10 3DF (tel: 09312 330). Mail order and export service for British miniatures. Catalogue: £2.50 (Visa/Mastercard).

Thames Valley Crafts, Mere House, Dedmere Road, Marlow, Bucks SL7 1PD (tel: 0628 890988). Mail order only, specialising in mini shops and accessories. Catalogue: £3 (Visa/Mastercard).

OVERSEAS SHOPS & DEALERS

Germany

Ilse Schweizer, Maxburgstrasse 4, 8033 München 2.

'Die Puppenstube', Valentinskamp 40/422000 Hamburg 36.

Das Puppenhaus, Unterstruth 61,6305 Grossen-Buseck.

'La Cassetta', Weberstrasse 126, 5300 Bonn 1.

Belgium

Lilliput Belgium, 59 Rue Colonel Van Gele, 1040 Bruxelles. (Miniatures association showroom/shop).

La Courte Echelle, 12 rue des Epéronniers, B-1000 Bruxelles.

Holland

'T Poppenspul, Oipoorstraat 61, 6981 DT Doesburg.

'T Torenhoekje, Bloemendaalseweg 165, 2061 CJ Bloemendaal.

Vanderpol Gifts, Oude Baan 61, 5244 JA Rosmalen.

Pommerijntje, Zwaanhals 333c, 3035 KK Rotterdam.

Poppe Goet Miniaturen, Schoolstraat 7, 3131 CW Vlaardingen.

De Speelmuis, Elandsgracht 58, 1016 TW Amsterdam.

France

French Miniatures Club & Magazine (Editor: Indeborg Riesser): Poupée Tendresse, 9 Rue Poussin, 75016 Paris

Corvinus, 16 rue des Halles, 75001 Paris.

Le Bouffon du Roi, 33 Avenue de Saint-Cloud, 78000 Versailles.

Boutique 'Miniatures', 16 rue Louis Maurel, 13001 Marseille.

Dolet Dolls' House, S. Leloup, 22 rue Etien Rougier & Plé, 13/15 bvd. des Filles du Calvaire, 75003 Paris. (Hobby materials shop & mail order catalogue)

Spain

'Puck', Duque de Sesto 30, Madrid 9. 'Puck' miniatures, toys & bookshop.

Drap, calle Pi No. 14, 08002 Barcelona.

Multicolor, Arenal 3, 28013 Madrid.

Kiddy-Dido, Plaza de San Jose 5, Bilbao.

Mundo de Max, Museo de la Miniatura, 03517 Guadalest, Alicante.

San Carlos, Becedo 7, Santander.

Denmark

'Smiths' Legetøj & Hobby, Vester Farimagsgade 1, 1606 København V.

Sweden

'Gyllene Katten', Dragarbrunnsg. 15, Box 2128, S 750 02 Uppsala.

'Glas & Grejor', Kolmätaregränden 9, S252 20 Helsingborg.

'Hökeriet', Lilla Torq 9, 21134 Malmö.

South Africa

V. A Harper, PO Box 3502, Symridge 1420.

Joep Suyker, 100 A Frances Road, Norwood 2192, Johannesburg. (Miniature construction)

Australia

Mary's Dolls' House, The Colonwoodes, Miller St, North Sydney, NSW.

'Houseworks', 229 Canterbury Rd, St. Kilda West, Victoria 3182.

Just Miniatures, Cnr Gladstone & Victoria Streets Hall, Canberra, ACT 2618. (Shop and mail order)

Miniature World, 12 Parliament Pl, West Perth, 6005. (Museum & shop)

Small Pleasures, 2 King's Place, Carlingford, NSW 2118.

Japan

Gran Papa, 2-9-24 Minami Aoyama, Minato-ku, Tokyo.

Bibliography

The following are life-size reference books to consult for making and furnishing period dolls' houses.

ANSCOMBE, Isabelle & GERE, Charlotte *Arts & Crafts in Britain & America 1880 onwards.* Academy Editions, London (1978)

AYRTON, Maxwell & SILCOCK, Arnold *Wrought Iron & its Decorative Use* Country Life, London (1929)

BANGERT, Albrecht *Thonet-Möbel* Wilhelm Heyne, Munich (1979)

BATSFORD, Harry & FRY, Charles *The English Cottage* Batsford, London (1938)

BAYERISCHES National Museum *Volkstümliche Möbel aus Altbayern* Deutsche Kunst Verl, Munich (1975)

BILLCLIFFE, Roger *Charles Rennie Mackintosh, the Complete Furnishings & Interior Designs* Lutterworth Press, Guildford & London (1986)

COOK, Olive *English Farmhouses & Cottages* Thames & Hudson, London (1982)

COOPER, Jeremy *Victorian & Edwardian Furniture & Interiors* Thames & Hudson, London (1987)

CRUICKSHANK, D. & WYLD, Peter *London: The Art of Georgian Building* Architect Book Publishing Co, New York (1975)

DAVIDSON, Caroline *The World of Mary Ellen Best* Chatto & Windus, London (1985)

DOWNING, A. Jackson *Victorian Cottage Residences* Dover Publications Inc, New York (1981)

DUFRENE, Maurice *Art Deco Interiors* Antique Collectors' Club, Woodbridge, UK (1989)

DUNCAN, Alastair *Art Deco* Thames & Hudson, London (1987)

EDWARDS, Ralph *Shorter Dictionary of English Furniture* Country Life/Hamlyn, London (1964)

EVANS, T. & LYCETT Green, C. *English Cottages* Weidenfeld & Nicolson, London (1982)

EVANS, Brill & LAWSOON, Andrew *A Nation of Shopkeepers* Plexus, London (1981)

FLEMING, John & HONOUR, Hugh *Penguin Dictionary of Decorative Arts* Viking, London (1989)

FRELINGHUYSEN, Alice Cooney *American Porcelain 1770–1920* Metropolitan Museum

GERE, Charlotte *19th Century Decoration* Weidenfeld & Nicolson, London (1989)

GIROUARD, Marc *Victorian Pubs* Yale, London (1984)

Glasgow School Of Art *Charles Rennie Mackintosh* Richard Drew Publications, Glasgow (1987)

GLOAG, John *Short Dictionary of Furniture* George Allen & Unwin, London (1952)

HERBERT, Janice S. *Oriental rugs* Macmillan, New York (1978)

HURRELL, J. *Measured Drawings of Old English Oak Furniture* Dover, New York (1983)

JEKYLL, Gertrude & JONES, Sydney *Old English Household Life* Batsford, London (1938)

LANDER, Hugh & RAUTER, Peter *English Cottage Interiors* Weidenfeld & Nicolson, London (1989)

MEISTER, Peter & REBER, Horst *European Porcelain of the 18th Century* Phaidon, London (1983)

MILLER, J. & M. *Period Details* Mitchell Beazley, London (1987)

MILLER, J. & M. *Period Style* Mitchell Beazley, London (1989)

PRAZ, Mario *An Illustrated History of Interior Decoration* Thames & Hudson, London (1964)

PRIZEMAN, John *Your House, the outside view* Quiller Press, London (1975)

ROTHCHILD, Mrs James de *The Rothchilds at Waddesdon Manor* William Collins, London (1979)

SEEBOHM, Caroline *English Country Living* Thames & Hudson, London (1987)

SERVICE, Alastair *Edwardian Interiors, poor, average & wealthy* Barrie & Jenkins, London (1982)

SPENCER, Charles *The Aesthetic Movement 1869–1890* Academy Editions, St Martins Press, London, New York (1973)

VAN DER KEMP, Gerald *Versailles* Sotheby Parke Bernet, London (1978)

TAYLOR, N. J. *Construction of Period Country Furniture* Stowbart & Sons, London (1978)

THORNTON, Peter *Authentic Decor 1620–1920* Weidenfeld & Nicolson, London (1984)

YARWOOD, Doreen *The English Home* Batsford, London (1979)

YARWOOD, Doreen *The British Kitchen* Batsford, London (1981)

YARWOOD, Doreen *The English Interior* Lutterworth, Guildford (1983)

Books About Antique Dolls' Houses

CHICAGO Art Inst. *The Thorne Min Rooms* Abbeyville Press, New York (1983)

DRÖSCHER, Elke *Puppenleben 1840–1930* (German) Bibliophile Taschenbücher, Dortmund (1982)

EARNSHAW, Nora *Collecting Dolls' Houses* Collins, London (1989)

GLUBOK, Shirley *Dolls' houses. Life in Min.* Harper & Rowe, New York (1984)

GREENE, Vivien *English Dolls' Houses* Batsford, London (1955)

GREENE, Vivien *Family Dolls' Houses* G. Bell & Sons, London (1973)

GRÖBER, Karl *Die Puppenstadt, 18th-century coll* (German) KR Langewiesche, Königstein GER

JACKSON, Valerie *Dolls' Houses & Miniatures* John Murray, London (1988)

JACOBS, Flora Gill *A History of Dolls' Houses* Charles Scribner's Sons, New York (1965)

JACOBS, Flora Gill *Dolls' Houses in America* Charles Scribner's Sons, New York (1974)

KING, Constance E. *Dolls & Dolls' Houses* Hamlyn, New York (1977)

KUNZ, Johanna *Schöne alte Puppenstuben* (German) Verlag Weingarten, Weingarten (1986)

LATHAM, Jean *Dolls' Houses, a personal choice* A&C Black, London (1969)

PIJZEL-DOMMISSE, J. *Het Poppenhuis (P de la Court's house in Utrecht Museum)* (Dutch) Veen/Reflex, Utrecht (1987)

REINELT, Sabine *Puppenküche u. Puppenherd,* (German) Verlag Weingarten, Weingarten (1987)

STEWART-WILSON, M. *Queen Mary's Dolls' House* Bodley Head, London (1988)

STILLE, Eva *Doll Kitchens, 1800–1980* Schiffer Publishing (1989)

WILCKENS, Leonie von *Mansions in Miniature* Viking Press, New York (1980)

Books on Making Dolls' Houses and Accessories

ATKINSON, Sue, *Making and Dressing Dolls' House Dolls* David & Charles (1992)

DAVENPORT, John *Making Miniature Furniture* Batsford, London (1978)

DODGE, Venus & Martin *Making Miniatures in 1/12th Scale* David & Charles, Newton-Abbot UK (1989)

HANKE, Ruth *Miniature House Plants* Craft/Plaid USA, Norcross (1979)

JOHNSON, Audrey *Furnishing Dolls' Houses* G. Bell, London (1972)

MCELROY, Joan *Dolls' House Furniture Book* A.A. Knopf, New York (1976)

MERRILL, Virginia & RICHARDSON, S. M. *Reproducing Period Furnishings and Accessories in Miniature* Crown Publications, New York (1981)

MERRILL, V. & JESSOP, Jean *Needlework in Miniature* Crown Publications, New York (1978)

MEYER, Barbara *Bread Dough Fruits and Vegetables* Craft/Plaid USA, Norcross (1977)

NEWMAN, Thelma & MERRILL, Virginia *The Complete Book of Making Miniatures* Crown Publications, New York (1975, reprinted 1989)

SMITH, Harry W. *Art of Making Miniature Furniture* Dutton, New York (1982)

WARNER, Barbara *Dolls' House Lighting* Boynton & Associates, Virginia (1986)

For reference books of interest to miniaturists and for dolls' house books, new and second hand, the oldest established specialist shop is: The Mulberry Bush, 25 Trafalgar St, Brighton, Sussex BN1 4EQ, England (tel: 0273 493781). Quarterly catalogue, Visa or Access, S.A.E. or International reply coupons with all enquiries please. Numerous historical booklets (ex 183 titles) are also available from: Shire Albums, Church St, Princes Risborough, Aylesbury HP17 8BR, UK.

Acknowledgments

My first thanks go to Jane, for her unfailing generosity in collaboration and in allowing me to treat her precious dolls' houses as an extension of my own collection. I would also like to thank my former Dollshouse Festival partner Sue Atkinson, Pam Cornish, Mr and Mrs EM Lee, and Barbara Speake for tolerating photographic invasions and the *International Dolls' House News'* Editor for the list of UK shops. My final thanks go to Patrick, 'The Infrastructure'.

The publishers wish to thank Aspect Picture Library for permission to use the pictures on pages 14, 120, 121 and 135.

Credits

The page numbers below refer to the pages where photographs appear.

PAGE 6: Architectural features by Borcraft Mouldings used by Kevin Mulvany. Left: an inlaid sewing table by John Davenport. Two ribband-back chairs and a walnut low table by John Hodgson. Lyre sofa table by Escutcheon. Arm chairs and harp home-made. Marble fire surround by Sussex Crafts. Lidded jars by Terry Curran. Firebasket by Alec Rothwell. Corner cupboard by Les Dunford. Spinet under window by John Otway. Clock and bracket by Alan Waters. Decoupage chest on stand by Ince to the Foot.

PAGES 18–19: Cottage by Hollycraft. Oak armchair, monk's chair, joint stool and venison meat by Wentways. Adam & Eve charger on mantel by Carol Lodder. Commonwealth chairs and oak gate-legged table by Escutcheon. Pewter by Philip Aitken. Stoneware by Terry Curran. Spit and firegrates by Terry McAlister. Onions by Bruce designs. Apples by Quality DH Miniatures. Spinning wheel from Wansbeck. Upstairs: antique chest from Mini Mansions. Reading chair Den Young. Cradle by John Finn. White quilt by Jay Harrison.

PAGE 20: Carpet by Mini Marvels. Plant stand from The Mulberry Bush with bowl by Rosalind Mercy. Furniture covered in striped silk by June Astbury. Tea set painted by Moorland Mins.

Dolls by Sunday Dolls. Fireplace by John Watkins. 'Bamboo' shelves by C & Y Roberson. Kitchen dresser by Impi. Washing machine by Bryntor. Ironing board by Geoff Barnett. Plate rack by Mulberry Bush. Art Nouveau carved bedroom furniture by Miren Tong. Bathroom suite by Sussex Crafts. Geyser by Basil Smetham.

PAGE 27: Bathroom fittings by Chrysnbon. Geyser by Sussex Crafts. David Edwards' back brush. Shaving brush and soap bowl by Terence Stringer. Razor and blades by Wentways. Alan Waters' shaving mirror. Turkish bath by Bryntor. Robe by Small World. Doll by Jill Nix.

PAGE 28: Highboy, chairs and candle stand from kits. Bookcase by Dennis Jenvey. Desk and mantelpiece by Impi. Frame by Unique Model galleon by Modelscape. Hanging candelabra from The Dolls House.

PAGE 29: Bonheur du jour desk, dropleaf table and firescreen by Dennis Jenvey. Home-made harp, piano and kit chairs. Roses by The Garden Path. Round table by Impi. Silver by Stuart McCabe, Gordon Blacklock, Sylvano Collection, Obadiah Fisher and Peter Acquisto. Bird cage and music stand by Alan Waters. Lute and tin record player by Jim Whitehouse. Clarebell chandelier with added glass beads. Pink lady by Little People. Harpist and girl by Jill Nix.

PAGE 58: Table and chairs by David Edwards. Child's high chair and armchairs by Ken Taylor. Chiffonier by Malcolm Chandler. Teaset on it by Avon. Kitchen range by Basil Smetham. Dresser and all its china by Rosalind Mercy. Small stool by Bishopstoke. Washstand by Jane Newman, the china by Linda Horsfall. Chair by David Booth. Quilt by Moorland Mins. The revarnished dressing table is from Taiwan. Ebony accoutrements by Terence Stringer. Flowers by Lyn Mitchell.

PAGE 61: Kitchen range and sewing machine by Phoenix models. Chairs by Ken Taylor. Peat bucket by R. Thrower. Plates by Bryntor. Toby teapot by Janice Crawley. Orkney chair and butterfly table by Rudeigin Beag. Chest by Malcolm Chandler. Sampler above it by Sue Mowat. Motto by Anchorage Miniatures.

PAGE 119: Patterned 'linoleum' paper by Sussex Crafts. Sewing table by Ron Brunsden. Jardinière bowl by Stokesay Ware. Plant by Jean Riggs. Screen by 'Rose Cottage'.

PAGE 133: 'Shamal' carpet commissioned. Silver sauceboat by Obadiah Fisher. Entrée dish by Stuart McCabe. Coaster and salt cellars by Gordon Blacklock. Red decanter by Albert Glass. 'China' by Rosamund Henley. Silverplate candelabra by Thames Valley Centrepiece by Lilliput Mins. Food by Country Treasures. Tureen by Holly Tree. 'Glasses' and cutlery by Chrysnbon.

Index